# THE ELIZABETHAN SERMON
## A SURVEY AND A BIBLIOGRAPHY

ALAN FAGER HERR

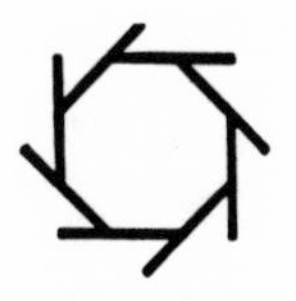

1969
OCTAGON BOOKS
*New York*

*Reprinted 1969*
*by special arrangement with Alan Fager Herr*

OCTAGON BOOKS
A DIVISION OF FARRAR, STRAUS & GIROUX, INC.
19 Union Square West
New York, N. Y. 10003



LIBRARY OF CONGRESS CATALOG CARD NUMBER: 77-75996

*Printed in U.S.A. by*
NOBLE OFFSET PRINTERS, INC.
NEW YORK 3, N. Y.

To

PRINCETON'S EDWARD HUBLER

Will not a filthy play with a blast of a trumpet sooner call a thousand than an hours tolling of the bell bring to the sermon an hundred?

—ARCHBISHOP SANDYS

# PREFACE

This study was undertaken when, stirred by the recent attention given by several editors to the excellent sermons of John Donne, and by T. S. Eliot to those of Lancelot Andrewes, I thought to look into the period immediately preceding to see whether the preaching of these Jacobeans was the continuation of a long tradition of fine sermons. At the very outset I was thwarted in my attempt by the complete lack of any bibliographies of the printed sermons preached in the reign of Elizabeth, and by the small and casual mention of all but a few important ones by the ecclesiastical historians. The *Short-Title Catalogue* was of great help in preparing a list from which to start reading, but its help thereafter diminished because of the very shortness of the titles, which rarely indicate whether a work with a religious-sounding title is a sermon, a commentary, a tract, a satire, or, as it fell out in several instances, a poem. Therefore, it appeared that the first step that should be taken in the field was the compilation of a bibliography which would not only list the sermons, but would set out rather full titles containing all given information about the sermons, their texts, dates, and the place and occasion of preaching. Such a bibliography I have compiled and here offer.

The bulk of this sermon literature is large; I have found about twelve hundred Elizabethan sermons in print. While some few of the preachers are represented by a large number of sermons, most of them published only one or two, and were men too unimportant to be included in any biographical collections. Therefore, in attacking these tens of thousands of pages of prose, by so many different hands, I have made no attempt, at the first general sally into the field, to evaluate each sermon or even each author severally. Instead, I have tried to survey the field as a whole, to indicate the range of the subject matter of the sermons, the manner in which they were preached, the reception they met with, and the course by which they came to be printed. I have not attempted to deal with the theology of the sermons except in the most obvious and unavoidable way. Finally, I have framed some tentative generalizations covering the more important literary aspects of the sermons to suggest their place in the whole body of Elizabethan prose. I venture to hope that the data here collected will prove useful to those who may wish to study the Elizabethan sermon more closely from the theological or the social point of view.

To Professor Matthias A. Shaaber I am heavily indebted for the great time, patience, and critical judgment he has bestowed on this study, and to Professors John C. Mendenhall, Matthew W. Black, and Alfred B. Harbage for their criticisms and suggestions. Beyond the walls of my own university, my thanks for the interest and encouragement of Professor Helen C. White and the many kindnesses of Regius Professor Claude Jenkins cannot be omitted on any account. I am grateful for the facilities put at my disposal by the librarians of the University of Pennsylvania, Philadelphia Divinity School, Union Theological Seminary, Bodleian Library, British Museum, Cambridge University, and by Librarian E. G. W. Bill of the Lambeth Palace Library.

A. F. H.

Moravian College
July 14, 1968

# CONTENTS

# CHAPTER I

## THE VOGUE OF THE SERMON

*Let a lawful and a godly seigniory look that they preach, not quarterly or monthly, but continually.*

THOMAS CARTWRIGHT

In the reign of Elizabeth the progress of preaching in England pursued a most erratic course. Sermons were alternately prohibited and enjoined, at all times subject to surveillance and criticism, while the preachers never knew what view of their preaching would be taken next. The age was a period of intense religious contention, and the confusion was kept in flux by the lack of any definite governmental stand. At the beginning of the reign the religious issue was quite simple; England would be either Roman Catholic or Protestant, the people thought, for Elizabeth was yet to demonstrate that there was a tenable middle ground. But the leniency by means of which Elizabeth hoped to reconcile all her subjects to the broad-based national church was interpreted as license to dissent from its usages at almost every point upon which divergence was possible and, once this spirit of dissent was well rooted, it was impossible to obtain conformity to any one corpus of dogma or usage.

As soon as the new Queen had been proclaimed, a furore in the pulpits began. The Protestants, suddenly free of the yoke of Mary, were loudly demanding a complete reformation and were further driven to outcry by seeing no great signs of action in that direction. The Roman Catholic party, apprehensive, feared that the Queen might tear down their newly reëstablished church and favor Protestantism. In their fervor both parties took great liberties in their sermons and assumed impertinent attitudes toward the Crown.

For a short time Elizabeth endured the confusion and then she saw the solution which could be found in the Bible: "Stay profane and vaine babblings, for they will increase unto more ungodlinesse".[1] On December 28, 1558, came the royal proclamation prohibiting all preaching until further notice.

> By the quene. The quenes majesty, understanding that there be certain persons, having in times past the office of ministery in the church, which now do purpose to use their former office in preaching and ministery, and partly have attempted the same; assembling, specially in the city of London, in sondry places, great nomber of people: whereupon riseth amonges the common sort not only unfruteful dispute in matters of religion, but also contention, and occasion to break common quiet: hath therefore, according to thauthoritie committed to her highness, for the quiet governaunce of all maner her subjects, thought it necessary to charge and commaund, like as hereby her highness doth charge and commaund all maner of her subjects, as well those that be called to ministery in the church, as all others, that they do forbear to preach or teach, or to gyve audience to any maner of doctrine or preachyng, other than to the gospels and epistels, commonly called the gospel and the epistel of the day, and to the Ten Commaundements in the vulgar tongue, without exposition or addition of any maner sense or meaning to be applyed or added; or to use any other maner of publick prayer, rite, or ceremony in the church, but that which is alredy used, and by law receaved; or the common letany used at this present in her majesty's own chappel, and the Lords Prayer, and the Crede in English; until consultation may be had by parlament, by her majesty, and her three estates of this realme, for the better conciliation and accord of such causes as at this present are moved in matters and ceremonies of religion.[2]

This sudden move disarmed everyone, but it was not received with bad grace since it was apparent that it would be wise to see just what position the Queen took on religious matters before one preached perhaps irretrievably in the wrong direction. Those who hoped soon to see where the Queen stood were disappointed; we do not know definitely to this day. Certain doctrines and usages Elizabeth approved of, and certain others she would not tolerate, but between these extremes lay vast theological territory undiscussed and ever uncertain. When sermons were again

---

1. *2 Timothy* 2:16.
2. Strype, *Annals*, vol. I, pt. 2, pp. 391-2.

permitted, preachers, remembering that there was danger in straying very far from approved doctrines, naturally tended to hew to the line of conformity in their sermons.

Sermons at the court never ceased even after the proclamation of silence, but they were preached by appointed stable and learned men on general topics not inciting controversy. On the first Sunday after Easter the public Paul's Cross sermons were resumed with the preaching of the customary Low Sunday Rehearsal Sermon even though on this occasion there had been no previous sermons to rehearse.[3] After this great public sermon, preaching began anew all over England as new licenses to preach were approved and issued by the bishops. Official licenses to preach had been required since 1548, and were of three degrees: [1] license to preach, [2] license to preach and to license, and [3] license to preach, to license, and to prohibit preaching. This system was calculated to reduce to a minimum all kinds of preachers and sermons unsavory to the civil and ecclesiastical authorities. Only clergy were licensed to preach, and to retain their clerical status they were required to subscribe to three main points of the established religion: first (1559) to the ecclesiastical supremacy of the Queen, later (1561) to the lawfulness of the *Book of Common Prayer* and the *Ordinal,* and finally (1603) to the thirty-nine *Articles of Religion.* With these prerequisites to admission to the ranks of the preaching clergy, there was a reasonable uniformity in the doctrine preached within the Established Church.

By the second act of Parliament in Elizabeth's reign people went to church under penalty of the law and listened to the sermons provided there.

> And that from and after the said Feast of the Nativity of St. John Baptist next coming, all and every Person and Persons inhabiting within this Realm, or any other and the Queen's Majesty's Dominions, shall diligently and faithfully, having no lawful or reasonable Excuse to be absent, endeavour themselves to resort to their Parish Church or Chapel accustomed, or upon reasonable Let thereof, to some usual Place where Common Prayer and such Service of God shall be used in such Time of Let, upon every Sunday, and other Days ordained and used to be kept as Holy Days, and then and there to abide orderly and

3. The nature of the Rehearsal Sermon is discussed below, p. 26. An account of the confusion attendant upon this particular occasion is contained in Sir John Hayward's *Annals of Q. Elizabeth,* Camden Soc. ed., p. 6.

soberly during the Time of the Common Prayer, Preaching, or other Service of God there to be used and ministered; upon Pain of Punishment by the Censures of the Church, and also upon Pain that every Person so offending shall forfeit for every such Offence twelve Pence, to be levied by the Churchwardens of the Parish where such Offence shall be done, to the Use of the Poor of the same Parish, of the Goods, Lands and Tenements of such Offender, by way of Distress.[4]

The archbishops, bishops, and diocesan ordinaries were charged to see this new law executed and to be answerable for any "Evils and Plagues" which God might send if this wholesome law were neglected. To put more teeth into the law, justices of oyer and determiner and justices of assize were empowered to enforce it with suitable civil punishments.

In the north, where Romanism had a stronger hold than elsewhere in England, recusants were obliged by law to attend even more services than were required of the general populace. Archbishop Whitgift of Canterbury inspired Archbishop Hutton of York to go beyond the church attendance law in his measures against the Romanists. Whitgift, in a letter to Hutton, thus hinted that something must be done:

Towching your self, I have not at anie time hard her Majestie to have apprehended anie complaintes against you, or to have conceaved otherwise then well of you; but here hathe bene informations gyven that recusants are of late increased in that province [York], and that you are to milde with them. Some of your ministers doe also affirme the same to be trewe.[5]

The stronger measures that were adopted in York were extra services consisting of a course of fifty sermons preached in defence of Protestant doctrine. The recusants attended the fifty sermons as they were required and, of course, most of them probably remained loyal Romanists.

It was a hard and thankless job to get all the recusants herded into church, but it was still more difficult to get them to listen closely to the sermons provided for their confutation. In 1591 Sir Richard Sherborne, with a touch of genius, thought of a way to avoid hearing the sermons, even though it was soon discovered. He and his family went to church when they were forced to go, but took the precaution to stuff wool in their ears so that they

---

4. Statutes, Anno Primo Reg. Eliz., Cap. II, Section XIV.
5. Hutton, *Correspondence,* letter LXXXIX.

heard nothing. Perplexed, the local authorities wrote to London for instructions in the case.[6]

Evasions of the church attendance laws must have been numerous, for to check up on the Sunday and Holy-day habits of an entire nation is plainly impossible. Then, too, the local parish officers who were to enter any complaints were usually not in haste to get their friends and neighbors into rather serious trouble with the impersonal powers of the canon and civil law. Even when people were quizzed on their church attendance, it was found that the questions could be evaded. The ways by which direct questioning was avoided are shown in the official directions as to the lawful manner of answering.

These questions being religious, a man should not give an answer dishonourable to God, as saying he goes to church, receives [the Sacrament], or has service, because he goes to Paul's, receives his rents, or has service of his men.[7]

Compared with the religious laws of other countries at this same time, these English laws and requirements of church attendance cannot be called harsh. People not in sympathy with the Church of England had only to put in an appearance at church or pay the fine, meanwhile believing what they pleased. The protection gained by paying the fine and the businesslike way in which the records of the fines were kept are shown in the following letter to Sir William More, Sir Thomas Browne, and others:

Where' Thomas Fryer, Doctor of Phisicke, dwellinge w'thin the Cytye of London, ys required by yo^r^ l're of this instante to be before youe at Dorkinge on Thurseday nowe next cominge, as touchinge his not cominge to Churche. It may please yowe to be advertised that the sayd Mr. Fryer hath ben allreddye called before the M^r^ of the Rolls and Sir Owyn Hopton, knighte, lieutenante of the Tower, Commissioners appoynted for the same cause, w'thin the Cyttie of London and the Countye of Midd. before whom he hath compounded and agreed to paye unto her Ma^tie^ a certen yearely some of money for his nott cominge to churche, as by the certyficate thereof, delyvered unto the Lordes of her Ma'ties pryvie councell, dothe appeare, w'ch by the comaundement of the M^r^ of the Rolls I am willed to signifie unto yo^r^ mastershipps. At London the xvii^th^ of Maye 1586. Yo^r^ w^r^shippes humbly to com'aunde, Henry Clerke, the Clarke of the Peace in the Countye of Midd.[8]

While it can be seen that people could avoid church atten-

6. *C.S.P.D. Elizabeth,* vol. CCXL, No. 140.
7. *C.S.P.D. Elizabeth,* vol. CCLXXIX, No. 90.
8. *Losely Manuscripts,* No. 99.

dance by dissembling or paying fines, the great majority went to church without grumbling or making an issue of it. With congregations provided by law to listen to its preachings, one might suppose that the Established Church would seize the advantage thus presented and pour forth a torrent of sermons, but it so fell out that there were far fewer than might be expected. The usual service consisted of Morning Prayer or Evening Prayer as prescribed in the *Book of Common Prayer* without the addition of a sermon. Preachers could preach as often as they would, for only a lower limit was set by authority. Four sermons a year were required, but even at these four occasions the 1559 *Common Prayer* allowed the preacher to substitute a reading from the *Book of Homilies* for the sermon. More than the four required sermons were expected, however, in all but the most wretched parishes. The frequency of sermons was from time to time regulated by injunctions issued by Elizabeth:

> If the person be able, he shall preach in his own person every month; or else shall preach by another, so that his absence be approved by the ordinary of the diocese, in respect of sickness, service, or study at the universities. Nevertheless, for want of able preachers and parsons, to tolerate them without penalty, so they preach in their own persons, or by a learned substitute, once in every three months of the year.[9]

Certain clergy there were who would not preach even four sermons a year without more compulsion than this. The Protestants were especially angry about this lack of zeal and termed the non-preaching clergy "dumb dogs". It became necessary to employ stronger measures to force these "dumb dogs" to preach the required sermons. Some ministers, of course, were merely too lazy to preach, but in most cases the neglect of sermons showed a leaning toward Catholicism and a consequent feeling that the Mass or Communion was the only important service of the church. Therefore the following order was issued in 1560:

> That at every communion there be a sermon. So may such as have quarter sermons have at every sermon a communion. And such as cannot or will not have preaching of the word in season and out of season, according to God's word, nor quarter sermons according to man's ordinance, shall not be allowed to abuse the seals of sacraments, according to their own affections and corrupt

9. From Bp. Cox's interpretation (1560) of the royal injunction. Strype, *Annals*, vol. I, pt. 1, p. 318.

customs. But they, by deferring of this sacrament to be ministered until doctrine be preached and received, may be thereby caused and occasioned more to desire and frequent preaching of the word. . . . Therefore when and whereas preaching wanteth, the people perish in their own sin, and their blood shall be required at the hands of those that have charge over them.[10]

While the government and the prelates favored and tried to enforce monthly or quarterly sermons, the very frequent sermons advocated by the most Protestant factions were not particularly desired by the authorities because they felt that the quality of sermons must certainly suffer if the preacher had to compose more than one sermon a month. Archbishop Whitgift has expressed his opinion of frequent preaching and ill-considered sermons:

But, if any hath said that some of those which use to preach often, by their loose, negligent, verbal, and unlearned sermons, have brought the word of God into contempt, or that four godly, learned, pithy, diligent, and discreet preachers might do more good in London than forty contentious, unlearned, verbal, and rash preachers, they have said truly, and their saying might well be justified.[11]

Thus it seems that the least valuable preachers preached most often, but the reason for this unfortunate state of the ministry may be seen in the disheartening response of the audiences to learned sermons. The predilection of Elizabethan audiences for the amusing and the sensational is no mere assumption, for the most zealous of the preachers speak of it as one of their greatest problems and discouragements. These complaints do not come only from the chronically ill-tempered ultra-Protestants who criticised everything indiscriminately; three bishops of the Church of England who were both able and willing preachers have recorded their views of their audiences. Archbishop Sandys tells of the popular attitude in one of his sermons.

The preacher is gladly heard of the people, that can carp the magistrates, cut up the ministers, cry out against all order, and set all at liberty. But if he shall reprove their insolency, pride, and vanity, their monstrous apparel, their excessive feasting, their greedy covetousness, their biting usury, their halting hearts, their muttering minds, their friendly words and malicious deeds, they will fall from him then. He is a railer, he doteth, he wanteth discretion.[12]

Sandys being an admittedly violent man, perhaps the view of tem-

10. Notes for the reformation of the ministry and the ministers (1560). Strype, *Annals,* vol. I, pt. 1, p. 315.

11. Whitgift, *Defence of the Answer to the Admonition,* tractate XI, division 3.

12. Sandys, *Works,* sermon 14, §22.

perate and learned Bishop Jewel should stand beside Sandys' outburst.

> Many are so ignorant, they know not what the scriptures are, they know not that there are any scriptures. They call them heretical and new doctrine. Many will believe neither side, whatsoever they allege. Bring they truth, bring they falsehood; teach they Christ, teach they antichrist; they will believe neither, they have so hardened their hearts. Be the preacher rough or gentle, learned or unlearned, let him use authority of the scriptures, of the doctors, of the councils, of decrees or decretals, of God's law, of man's law, nothing will move them, nothing will please them; because the ministry of God, and thereby God himself, is despised.[13]

This disappointment in the attitude of the congregations on the part of the clergy was rather widespread, and it was naturally reflected in the quality of the sermons as well as their quantity. Bishop Babington was so disheartened at the response of his audiences that he despaired of having any effect on them. Having prayed after a sermon, he concluded thus: "And Amen say I againe to this Prayer, leaving you now to your liberty to go forwards with other temptations as you will."[14]

Another factor which helped to thwart the intention of the laws that enjoined frequent sermons was the state of the clergy, for the number of Elizabethan clergy able to preach a good learned sermon was not only limited, but in reality very small indeed. The quality of the clergy, at least in the beginning of the reign, was very poor. Moreover, there was the further defect that the ranks of the clergy were unhappily very much depleted.

Only two of the old Marian bishops remained to carry on into the reign of Elizabeth, the others having either died or been deposed for not conforming to the new doctrines of the Church or for not acknowledging Elizabeth as the head of the Church of England. The new bishops cannot be called either unlearned or unfitted for their posts, but it was a long time before their ranks were filled up. This delay was aggravated by the fact that Elizabeth received the incomes from all offices while they were vacant, and she was in no hurry to appoint men to fill the financially pleasant

---

13. *Sermon of Psalm LXIX:9* (*Works,* II, 1014).
14. *Works,* ed. of 1637, p. 199.

vacancies.[15] The number of the lower clergy who fled from their posts at the time of the changing of religion or who were deprived of office by the new regime is not known with any certainty,[16] but it is certain that there was a great lack of men of the right calibre in the lower clergy and that replacements were difficult to make. The universities were not able to turn out enough men trained for the priesthood even to begin to fill the vacancies, and so, pressed by the great need, the bishops filled the most crying gaps in the ranks with the next best men they could find, and left the less important vacancies unfilled or in the hands of lay readers. This condition was only a temporary one, but one that limited the number and the quality of the sermons preached. The men who were not fitted to preach properly were not licensed to preach, while the licensed preachers were sent about the parishes to supply occasional sermons and thus to distribute the preachers as widely as possible. Even bishops condescended to go about preaching like the lower clergy, so great was their desire to serve the needs of the Church.

Under these circumstances the *Book of Homilies* assumed new importance. As an emergency move to provide services in parishes that were now without preachers, a substitute order of laymen known as "readers" was installed. Readers could read from the *Book of Common Prayer* or the *Book of Homilies* without any chance of propagating doctrine contrary to that of the Established Church. The activity of readers beyond this was limited; they could not preach, nor administer the sacraments, but they could bury the dead and conduct the service of the churching of women after childbirth. These readers did not give over their accustomed occupations, and by the same token did not receive the full stipend that was attached to the office in which they were substituting, but only such part of it as the bishop or ordinary of the diocese thought meet and proper. Readers were not appointed from any particular station or walk in life, but it was ordained that

> Any that liveth honestly upon any vocation, and, in the absence of a minister,

---

15. See *C.S.P.D. Elizabeth,* vol. VII, No. 19, concerning delays in consecrations to the sees of Canterbury, London, Ely, Hereford, and Chichester.

16. W. H. Frere, in *The English Church in the Reigns of Elizabeth and James I,* p. 104, estimates that not more than 200 were deprived.

can and will read any thing appointed to be read, only of good will to serve the parishioners, may be permitted.[17]

This *Book of Homilies* from which priests and readers read was composed in the reign of Edward VI and was issued in 1547. It contained twelve homilies, the small number of which made repetitions frequent. In the epilogue of the book a second volume was promised and the tentative titles of the homilies were listed. In the convocation of 1562 the bishops decided to provide these promised homilies and they prepared them among themselves. This second volume did not contain all of the homilies proposed by the first volume, such as those against covetousness, envy, anger, and malice, but it did contain others not promised to a total of twenty. This second volume was printed in 1563 with a preface by Bishop Cox containing the Queen's rules governing the use of the homilies:

All which Homilies, Her Majesty commandeth, and straightly chargeth all Parsons, Vicars, Curates, and all other having Spiritual cure, every Sunday and Holy-day in the year, at the ministring of the holy Communion, or if there be no Communion ministred that day, yet after the Gospel and Creed, in such order and place as is appointed in the Book of Common Prayers, to read and declare to their Parishioners plainly and distinctly one of the said Homilies, in such order as they stand in the Book, except there be a Sermon.[18]

Again in 1569 the six parts of the *Homily Against Rebellion* were added on the occasion of the disorders in the North, bringing the total number of homilies to thirty-three.

All of these homilies were for the whole Church of England, but Bishop Cooper, in 1580, composed one more homily and ordered its use in his own diocese of Lincoln. This homily was prepared for one particular occasion:

A brief Homily, wherein the most comfortable and right use of the Lords Supper, is very plainly opened and delivered, even to the understanding of the unlearned and ignorant. Made to be used throughout the Diocesse of Lincolne, before everie celebration of the Lordes Supper, in all such Churches and Parishes as have not a sufficient hable Preacher allowed under the hand and authentike seal of the Bishop there, and to be read by the Minister of each such place, so distinctly and in such sorte, that all wich shal be then assembled, may well heare and marke the same.[19]

---

17. Notes for the reforming of the ministry etc. (1560). Strype, *Annals*, vol. I, pt. 1, p. 314.
18. Preface to the 1563 ed. of *The Second Tome of Homelyes*.
19. Part of the title of the edition of 1580.

On the other hand, the fact that people balked at attending sermons when that attendance was forced and the fact that they behaved with less propriety than is expected of a sermon audience today must not be taken to indicate that sermons were generally unpopular with either clergy or laity. Before the reformation churches did not have the rarefied and inhibiting atmosphere that is apparent in many today; people felt quite at home in church and behaved accordingly. The Elizabethans were interested in religion and delighted in discussions of it, the subject then not being taboo in conversation. A man as worldly as Thomas Nashe would set himself up as a sermon critic, and a man as busy as John Manningham would be a connoisseur of the art of preaching and would fill his diary with very full notes of sermons he had heard and his critical judgments of them. Lady Margaret Hoby would make the tedious and uncomfortable journey from Yorkshire to London to hear her favorite preacher, Stephen Egerton, whose congregation for some reason consisted mostly of women.

Neither were all the clergy apathetic in the matter of preaching. Some, besides feeling that it was their duty, took delight in preaching; a few even delivered two sermons on Sundays and lectured on certain week-days. But most of the frequent preachers were those who belonged to the Protestant wing of the Church or were without the Church in the ranks of the ultra-Protestants. Cartwright, the eminent Presbyterian, within the Established Church, not only was in favor of unceasing sermons, but had strong objections to infrequent sermons that had taken months to prepare:

> Those that go long with a sermon, and which I know, and have heard, when they come to bring it forth, bring forth oftentimes more wind and unprofitable matter than any good and timely fruit, or wholesome substantial doctrine.[20]

The zealots who most wanted preaching were the very ones who had been prohibited to congregate and hear sermons; in this group fell the Brownists, the Puritans, the Barrowists, the Family of the Mount, the Family of Love, the Essentialists, and the Anabaptists. But in spite of threatenings and prohibitions under penalty of law, the forbidden assemblies of these unauthorized sects were

---

20. *An Answer to the Admonition,* tractate XI.

held furtively in private houses and isolated fields and woods. These secret meetings were at first merely for prayer and meditation, but gradually they came to be focal points of the agitation for the overthrow of the Established Church. It is doubtful, however, whether the Puritans at this time considered themselves schismatics with the other sects; more likely they intended only to constitute a movement within the Church. All of these strongly Protestant sects were given to congregational participation in the exposition of scriptural texts. At the meeting of a secret congregation there would be a sermon and then open discussion, and frequently there was also the giving of personal testimony. This type of prohibited service was known as "prophesying" and was prohibited on the grounds that the preaching was not being done by licensed preachers. Moreover, to the horror of the episcopate, the Family of Love and certain other sects allowed and encouraged women to preach and expound. A tamer variety of prophesying was found within the Established Church, but since in this case the sermons were preached by men licensed to preach by the bishops, the practice there was only discouraged.

While the secret congregations did have sermons, the sermons were not considered ends in themselves, but rather as encouragements to more perfect godliness. The subject matter of such sermons was rarely anything mystical or erudite; usually it was exhortation concerning conduct and the appeasing of an angry God. Even the capable and famous Puritan preacher John Knewstub was praised by his fellows more for his prayers than for his sermons. The meetings of the congregations being secret, there is very little first hand evidence of the nature of those meetings. There is, of course, the minute book of the Dedham classis, but this does not much concern the sermons of the dissenters since the classes were not regular congregations, but rather groups of clergymen who met to meditate, fast, pray, and plot together. The forbidden sermons were not printed because of the risk to the printer involved and also because publication would only gain the sects unwanted publicity and consequent investigation.

Together with the ultra-Protestants, the Romanists were also forbidden to preach, but preach they did and that quite openly at times. Father Campion of the Society of Jesus preached at Smithfield in 1580 while there was a reward posted for his apprehension. There is a record of another Roman sermon preached just as openly, but not with equal impunity.

> On Monday there was a great assemblie of men and women of this towne [London] at the Marshalsee to heare a Scottish Frier Capuchin preach, where they were staide and kept all night to the number of three or fowrescore, and afterwards examined by the Bishop of London, Dr. Stanhop and others. Some were dismissed payenge theyre charges, some bound over, and some committed.[21]

The cleverest of the Roman preachers was Thomas Heth, S. J., brother to the late Archbishop of York, who employed subtle strategy in his preaching. For six years he went about preaching openly in churches with the permission and even by the appointment of the ordinaries of the dioceses; the reason for his great success was his disguise as a wandering preacher with Puritan leanings. The sudden end of his preaching came like the dénouement of a third-rate melodrama; during a sermon in Rochester Cathedral approved by the Dean, papers of identification fell out of his pocket and were retrieved by the sexton, who scuttled off to the Bishop with them. The rest of the story is one of the pillory, cutting off of ears, nose-slitting, forehead-branding, and life imprisonment.[22]

In any event, these prohibited sermons of either Protestants or Romanists were but a small proportion of all the sermons preached. The great majority of the people did attend the Church of England services and willingly listened to the sermons provided there. In fact, they attended sermons where there was no other service and no compulsion, as at St. Mary's Hospital (known more simply as the "Spittle") or at Paul's Cross. That people attended these sermons willingly does not, however, imply that they attended in any particularly pious frame of mind, as will be seen later.

Paul's Cross had a long tradition of preaching behind it even before John Colet, becoming Dean of St. Paul's in 1505, estab-

21. Chamberlain, *Letters*, vol. I, p. 90.
22. Strype, *Annals*, vol. I, pt. 2, p. 272-3.

lished regular sermons there every Sunday and holy-day. These sermons were preached from a pulpit set up in the churchyard in a corner formed by the chancel and the transept. In the event of inclement weather the preaching was moved indoors to a chapel under the choir of the cathedral or, as during the rebuilding of St. Paul's after the fire of 1562, to the Grey Friars (Christ's Church).

The sermons at Paul's Cross, and perhaps at a few other pulpits, were frequently made more amusing for the audience by the exhibition of people doing penance. At the Cross there was a regular platform, level with the pulpit, built for the penitents to stand upon and receive the jeers of the audience and the gibes of village wits. Sometimes the penitents simply stood up throughout the sermon and were considered amply punished. While Dean Nowell preached on February 10, 1560, a man thus stood up for committing bigamy.[23] More spectacular was the man who stood wrapped in a sheet during the sermon of November 6, 1561, for charging Veron, the Rector of St. Martin's, with incontinency, and on the 23rd of the same month another man was more deeply humiliated by being forced to kneel and beg Veron's pardon for circulating a rumor that Veron had been "taken with a wench".[24] Public penance before the huge jeering audience of the Cross was a very powerful weapon against scandal and was often resorted to. It might be added that the distraction of these side-shows was probably a great hindrance to the preacher's efforts to hold the attention of his audience.

These Paul's Cross sermons were probably the most important in London because of the size of the audience, which was only limited by the power of the preacher's lungs. These audiences are estimated to have been as large as six thousand. It was not only a huge audience, but a most mixed one, since not only the common people gathered there, but also many nobles and officers of the court and the city attended with full ceremony and retinue. Here the great preachers held forth by invitation and

23. Strype, *Annals*, vol. I, pt. 1, p. 297.

24. *Ibid.*, vol. I, pt. 1, pp. 406-7. This form of penance was not an innovation of the reign of Elizabeth. For example, in 1556 a man who broke the Lent laws stood with two pigs on his head (Machyn, *Diary*, p. 101).

visiting clergy from all over England were heard. The excellence of the preachers varied with the season, for the prelates occupied the pulpit mostly during the sessions of Parliament, at which time they would be in London to sit in the House of Lords. The special care given to selecting preachers in this season can be seen from this letter from Bishop Grindal to Dr. Hutton:

Salutem in Christo! Wheras I appoynted you to preache att Paules Crosse the 3 off November nexte: becawse the Parlament dothe holde, and therfore it is lyke that the Bisshops shall occupie the rowme those Sundays in the myddes off the tearme, I muste entreate you to prevente your daye, and to preach Dominica 17ª, which is the 6 off October nexte. The tyme, thowghe it may be somewhatt shorte, is longe enoughe for you; and I am destitute. It is the firste Sundaye off the Parlament, and therfore I labour to have one learned for thatt daye. I praye you fayle nott, and certiffie me wth conveniente spede agayne. Fare ye well.[25]

At other times of the year there was a great variety of preachers ranging from dull to sensational, ignorant to learned, and Protestant to Anglo-Catholic.

The appointment of the preachers to this important pulpit originally lay with the Bishop of London and the Dean of St. Paul's, but by Elizabeth's reign a great number of authorities, as well civil as ecclesiastical, exercised this perogative. This thus dispersed authority accounted for many untoward preachings and ridiculous occurrences. When, in 1564, Thomas Samson the Puritan and Lawrence Humphrey, another Puritan whom Bishop Jewel had refused ordination, were being held in custody in London for preaching without proper episcopal license, their names appeared on the list of Paul's Cross preachers. The Queen was incensed, but by the time she found that it was not the Bishop of London, nor the Lord Mayor, nor her secretary who had appointed them, but the Earl of Leicester, there was no time to appoint substitutes and so these two men had the immense pleasure of preaching openly at the most coveted pulpit in England while they were in custody for their offensive preaching.[26] At other times ill-chosen men spent their hour in this great pulpit flaying the Established Church and then fled until the hue and cry died down. Though the laws were strict, it was difficult to check

25. Hutton, *Correspondence,* letter II.
26. Strype, *Annals,* vol. I, pt. 2, pp. 132 ff.

upon all the sermons in London and then act swiftly enough to apprehend the offenders. Taking advantage of this situation, preachers in great pulpits, small pulpits, and forbidden pulpits grew bold. When Elizabeth once reproved the Bishop of London for indiscretions of some ministers in and about London, the Bishop excused himself on the ground that the churches and pulpits in London were so many that Argus himself could not keep watch over all of them.[27]

A less troublesome public pulpit was that at St. Mary's Spittle, which was important in Easter week only. This open air pulpit was placed in the churchyard adjoining St. Mary's Hospital, in Bishopsgate Ward, and had, besides a great space for the audience to stand in, a two-storied building the windows of which accommodated the prelates, Lord Mayor, aldermen, and sheriffs of the city.[28] Annually sermons were preached at this pulpit on Easter Monday, Tuesday, and Wednesday by especially appointed learned preachers, often of episcopal rank. These three sermons together with the Good Friday sermon at Paul's Cross were critically reviewed and an original sermon added in a spectacular preaching held at the Cross on Low Sunday. This long and difficult review sermon was known as the "Rehearsal Sermon", and because of its difficulty and importance was always preached by a carefully chosen man. These Eastertide sermons were attended with considerable ceremony; the mayor and aldermen came wearing violet on Good Friday and Easter Wednesday and scarlet on Easter Monday and Tuesday and on Low Sunday. A huge audience of common people naturally assisted at such celebrated and colorful occasions.

Besides going to the cathedral to transact business, to meet friends, to see some person pay off a wager by hopping in a sack, or to watch a man ride a horse on the top of the steeple,[29] people went there to hear the many sermons and week-day lectures delivered by the cathedral staff, which consisted of "a Deane, a

27. See the letter of Dr. Ed. Stanhope to Sir John Stanhope, December 29, 1599, printed in *C.S.P.D. Elizabeth,* vol. CCLXXIII, No. 59.

28. For a full description of the Spittle see John Stow's *Survey of London,* ed. by C. L. Kingsford, I, 166 ff.

29. Chamberlain, *Letters,* p. 102.

chaunter, a chauncelor, a Treasurer, 5. Archdeacons, . . . and 30. prebendaries".[30] There were also 123 parish churches in London and its immediate suburbs,[31] and many of the clergy of these churches had large and enthusiastic followings. At St. Anne's Blackfriars, Stephen Egerton preached to his predominantly female congregation; at St. Andrewes Holborn, one could hear Richard (afterward Archbishop) Bancroft or Dr. John King; at St. Giles Cripplegate, Lancelot Andrewes; at Christ Church, Newgate, Richard (afterward Bishop) Greenham; and at St. Clement Danes, Henry Smith. These and other eminent clergymen were highly esteemed and at sermon time their churches were filled and the overflow, trying to catch what words they could, filled the porches and steps.[32] Of Dr. King, whom King James termed "the King of Preachers",[33] Manningham says "He is soe highly esteemed of his auditors, that when he went to Oxford they made a purse for his charges, and at his return rode forth to meete him, and brought him into towne with ringing, etc."[34] Others of the popular clergy were not the most sound theologically nor necessarily the most sincere, but those who were most sensational or "jolly" as Dr. William Alley was termed. A large proportion of the audience went to these men not to learn nor to be inspired, but to be amused.

The Elizabethans were not only pleased to listen to sermons, and those much longer than present day sermons, but they also read sermons in print for pleasure and for edification. The sale of printed sermons was encouraging to the printers and as a result publications of sermons increased steadily throughout the reign. By decades they increased thus:

| | | | |
|---|---|---|---|
| 1560-1570 | 9 | 1580-1590 | 113 |
| 1570-1580 | 69 | 1590-1600 | 140 |

This tabulation, made from the appended bibliography, which includes, I believe, a very large majority of the Elizabethan sermons which got into print, is not of individual sermons, but of

30. Stow, *Survey of London*, II, 137.
31. *Ibid.*, II, 143.
32. Manningham, *Diary*, p. 75.
33. Wood, *Athenae Oxonienses*, I, pp. 457-9.
34. *Op. cit.*, p. 79.

volumes, and it does not include the numerous translations of continental divines that were published and widely sold in England. Even as early as 1577 the popularity of printed sermons was such that it occasioned this comment:

> Amongest the innumerable varietie of Bookes that are published in these our dayes . . . I suppose ther be none (next after the holy & sacred Scriptures) that are either for profit or pleasure, more greedily to be imbraced of the Godly, than those that conduce as well to the understanding of the Propheticall and Apostolick writings, as also to the furtheraunce and practise of that knowledge that is gotten out of the same.[35]

And not only the "godly" bought and read sermons, but the casual readers as well; they were not published simply for the edification of other clergy, nor as a source to crib from. Sermons that had been preached on important occasions (and these occasions were secular as well as religious, as will be seen further on) had large sales because they were usually by high-ranking clergy, as the occasion demanded, and also, since the people were interested in the sort of sermon that would be preached before the Queen, at a social function that they could not attend, or at the funeral of a personage whom they either dearly loved or hotly hated, because these sermons had a certain news value. Sometimes it was the preacher's name that sold the sermons. Henry Smith's sermons went into a phenomenal number of editions and his name on a sermon was so attractive to buyers that it was charged that unscrupulous printers forged sermons over his name when they could not lay their hands upon authentic copy.[36]

Thus it is apparent that the sermon had a considerable vogue throughout the age of Elizabeth. Preaching was enjoined upon the clergy by the ecclesiastical authorities and the law provided them with audiences to hear their discourses. The reluctance of lackadaisical and disaffected ministers to preach as required was to some extent offset by the fervor of those with evangelical leanings whose zeal bade them to preach on any and every occasion; the lack of qualified ordained preachers, in the early part of the reign, was in part compensated for by volunteer teachers of the Word who, at the risk of severe punishment, expounded the

35. Gerardus, *Practis of Preaching,* 1577 translation, sig. A2 recto.
36. See the full title of Henry Smith's *Jacob's Ladder.*

gospel in irregular and clandestine assemblies. The preaching of a sermon was often a festive occasion and was always followed with an interest unabashed by the frigidity which passes for good manners in polite congregations today. Moreover, the Elizabethan sermon deals even more freely than the sermon of today with topics not specifically religious. Sermons will be discussed later that deal with local and international politics, the social and economic plight of the poor, charges of scandal in the clergy, vitriolic feuds within the clergy, famous and sensational trials, the question of the Queen's successor, spectacular fires, facts every pregnant woman should know,[37] the ravages of recent plagues, and even the inconsistency of the weather. As the age of Elizabeth was more religious — which is not to say more pious — than our own, the Elizabethan sermon was naturally more vital and more eagerly attended.

37. See full title of Christopher Hooke's *The Child-birth or Woman's Lecture.*

# CHAPTER II

## PULPIT DELIVERY

*How he stampt and tooke on I cannot tell, but crash quoth the pulpit, and there lay Hubberdin sprawling in the middest of his audience.*

JOHN FOXE

Delivering a sermon in Elizabethan days was not so tame an undertaking as it is today. The difficulties were many, and at times overpowering.

Before the preacher even mounted the pulpit steps the problem of vestments or habits had to be considered. So high was the feeling on this controversial point that no matter what the preacher wore or left unworn, somebody would find fault. The most Protestant of the clergy had refused to wear the prescribed habits, but Archbishop Parker had, on March 26, 1566, called the London clergy together and ordered them either to "were theyr aparayll accordyng to ye quens injunctions, or ells to do no sarvyce".[1] If the preacher wore the habit prescribed by the Queen and the bishops, he would be accused by the Protestants of favoring Rome, and protests would be loud against his "popish rags". On April 7, 1566, the parish of St. Mary Magdalen in Milk Street asked the bishop to appoint a minister to celebrate Holy Communion for them. The minister came and wore a surplice, as he was instructed to do by the bishop. The sight of this surplice so enraged a member of the congregation that, after the minister had

1. Stow, *Memoranda,* p. 135.

come down from the altar to read the epistle and gospel of the day, he sent his servant up behind the minister's back to seize and run off with the chalice of wine and the paten of bread! Holy Communion was that day precipitately discontinued.[2] If the minister had appeared in ordinary clothes to please such people, he would have had to answer for disobeying the Queen and the bishops.

Another hindrance to the preacher was the use of churches as secular meeting places. For all of Bishop Pilkington's charges that in the days of Roman Catholic administration the temple had been polluted by business and brawling, it was no better in Elizabeth's reign. People still had to have their ears nailed to a post and then cut off for fighting in St. Paul's,[3] and that cathedral was still a great business center and social promenade. The fact that a service might be in progress did not stop the other activities; even as late as 1602, after forty-four years of reforming, the shutting of the doors of St. Paul's during services brought about at least one preserved objection that this practice deranged the traffic of news. When John Chamberlain wrote to Dudley Carleton in November of that year he had little to tell him because of that innovation:

> My last to you was of the fourth or fift of this present, since which time here hath ben a very dull and dead terme, or els I am quite out of the trade, which may well be, by reason of a new devised order to shut the upper doores in Powles in service time, whereby the old entercourse is cleane chaunged, and the trafficke of newes much decayed.[4]

A seemingly popular diversion that was sure to distract a preacher and his audience during service was to sing lustily out of turn. W. Fleetwood, the recorder, in a letter to Lord Burghley, tells of an arraignment of a young hoodlum for such an offence, the charge being the disturbance of the peace:

> Light [the defendant whom Fleetwood thought was "descended of the blood of Nero the tiraunt"] is specially indicted for singing in the churche on Childer-

2. Stow, *Memoranda,* p. 136.
3. Strype, *Annals,* vol. I, pt. 1, p. 407.
4. *Letters,* vol. I, p. 171.

mas Day, "fallantida dillie," &c.[5] My Lord Bishop was at the arraignment of Light. Light confessed all that he was charged with.[6]

If such an offence drew a bishop to the arraignment, the following incident must have seemed far more grievous:

It happened in February this year [1572], in the parish church of St. Simon [Norwich], (a parish noted for their disorders,) at evening prayer, after the minister had begun, and proceeded to the midst of the service, reading the Psalms distinctly to the people; three or four lewd boys, set on by some lewder persons, (whether they were papists, or protestants disaffected to the liturgy,) came into the church, and as the said minister began to read, *My soul doth magnify the Lord,* &c. they brast out into singing of psalms suddenly and unlooked for; and being commanded by the minister to cease, they continued singing, and he reading; so as all was out of order, and the godly, well-disposed auditors there disquieted and much grieved.[7]

Besides the intrusion of the people not intending to be present at the service and people bent on perpetrating outrage, the attitude of the ordinary congregation was distracting enough to the preacher. The church edifice was given no particular reverence and the congregations were restrained by no inhibitions in their behavior there. One minister felt that he should remark on this from the pulpit.

Further, Gods house is abused by them which bring hither hawks and dogs, which is faulted in our Church-homilie, and whereby peoples mindes are diverted from their devotions.[8]

This same preacher protests against persons in the congregation lying down to rest in the church, tearing the clothes off brides, laughing when marriage banns are read, or talking business, and against those who come to church to show off their new clothes and "seem to march as if they would exactly measure out the earth by their mincing, or else leade some pompous train upon the stage."[9]

---

5. This "fallantida dillie" was not a secular refrain, but probably part of the Christmas or Epiphany carol *Out of the orient crystal skies,* the last stanza of which is:

> The shepherds dwelling there about,
> When they this news did know,
> Came singing all even in a rout,
> 'Falan-tiding-dido!'

This carol will be found in the *Oxford Book of Carols.*

6. Wright, *Queen Elizabeth and her Times,* II, 184-5.
7. Strype, *Annals,* vol. II, pt. 1, pp. 328-9.
8. Robert Shelford, *A Sermon of Gods House,* p. 54.
9. *Ibid.,* p. 47.

Not only was the church building given thus little reverence, but the clergy were accorded no more. If a congregation became so incensed at a preacher as to want to manhandle him, his cloth could not be counted upon to save him. We hear of a preacher in the troublesome see of Chester who was put in the stocks by unauthorized persons and pelted with rotten eggs by the women of the parish because, at the instigation of his bishop, he had preached a Protestant sermon in this Catholic-minded diocese. An assault on a preacher due to his vestments is recorded by John Stow, the historian:

> On the 3 day of June [1566], beynge Whitson Monday, at nyght, ye Scott (who before had ussyd to preche at S. Magnus and so sore to envey agaynst ye capps, syrplisis, and suche lyke) did servys at S. Margaret Pattyns in Roode Lane, wher he ware a syrplice; and a sertayne nonbar [sic] of wyves threw stons at hym and pullyd hym forthe of ye pulpyt, rentyng his syrplice and scrattyng his face, &ct.[10]

David Dee, pastor of Sherborne, Dorset, fared no better at the hands of his parishioners. They set upon him, pulled the hairs out of his beard, and so "fisted" him that he could not speak loud enough to preach for six weeks.[11] It is plain that a preacher might do well to consider the congregation's reaction as he stood in his pulpit.

At Paul's Cross the preacher had one or more companions in the pulpit with him; we might almost call them "seconds" when we consider the preacher's need of protection if he displeased too large a portion of the audience. Despite the presence of guards to keep the peace, daggers might be thrown, as happened early in the reign of Mary when Gilbert Bourne preached a sermon wherein he defended Bishop Bonner. Bourne's companion in the pulpit rose and caught the dagger in his sleeve.[12] There was also the possibility that the pulpit might be stormed if the customary coughing and heckling seemed too mild a rebuke to an unpopular preacher. A type of protest against the sermon that was far more acceptable to the preacher took the form of writing objections on paper and throwing them into the pulpit. This was

10. *Memoranda*, p. 139.
11. 1582. *C.S.P.D. Elizabeth*, vol. CLII, No. 35.
12. See Machyn, *Diary*, p. 41, and Stow, *Annales*, pp. 613-4.

not considered a breach of the peace and so was allowed.

Even though the hindrances and difficulties were what they were, Elizabethan audiences expected to hear sermons which satisfied their criteria. The least of the preacher's worries was the fact that there would be protests if he read his sermon, because if it were read it would not fulfil their definition of a sermon. In Elizabeth's day the distinction between a sermon and a lecture was not what it is today; if a spoken discourse is didactic and upon dogmatic theology we are likely to term it a sermon and if it is upon scientific or other secular matter we call it a lecture, whereas the Elizabethans termed a theological discourse a lecture or a sermon depending only upon whether it was read from a finished composition or preached from memory with the aid of notes only. This distinction was rigidly preserved in the titles when the sermons and lectures went to the press. A further distinctive term was reserved for a theological dissertation which was neither preached nor read before an audience; this was called a treatise. When a man came to preach a sermon, therefore, he endeavored to use only notes and to have those notes as brief as possible. To preach without even the notes was the aspiration. The fullness or brevity of the notes from which the sermon was to be delivered was a matter of choice for the preacher. Very few of those notes have been published, naturally enough, but we may presume that they varied in length as greatly as do men's memories. Bishop Andrewes' notes were full to the point of indicating the nature of nearly every sentence,[13] while Hooker used none at all.

The Elizabethan clergy were allowed more time to present their sermons than most churches grant their clergy today, for while we are content with even a quarter-hour sermon, then both the congregation and the preacher felt that one hour was meet and right for sermon length. Lest any contention arise about the matter, we find that the congregation did not disdain to provide an

13. Notes for sermons that Andrewes did not preach are published with his other works in the *Library of Anglo-Catholic Theology*.

hour-glass nor the clergy to turn it over as they mounted the pulpit steps.[14]

Gestures were expected to accompany a good strong sermon. So usual were they, as a matter of fact, that there is very little mention of them in contemporary discussions of sermons, except to note anything so unusual as the lack of them. Hooker, for example, stood in his pulpit motionless, not even moving his eyes, and this idiosyncrasy was considered remarkable enough to appear in every account of that great preacher. Since Elizabethan sermon audiences preferred everything else in its most sensational form, it is not taking too much for granted to suppose that they liked their pulpits well pounded.

Most important in sermon delivery was the clarity and carrying power of the preacher's voice, and the congregations did not hesitate to complain if they could not hear properly. John Manningham was a competent sermon critic and a careful note-taker, so that he was especially disappointed at poor delivery. He recorded a disappointment in his diary:

> In the afternoone Mr. Marbury of the Temple, text xxi. Isay. 5v. &c. But I may not write what he said, for I could not heare him, he pronounces in manner of a common discourse. Wee may streatche our eares to catch a word nowe and then, but he will not be at the paynes to strayne his voyce, that wee might gaine one sentence.
>
> I love not to heare the sound of the sermon, except the preacher will tell me what he says. I thinke many of those which are fayne to stand without dores at the sermon of a preacher whom the multitude throng after may come with as greate a devotion as some that are nearer, yet I beleeve that most come away as I did from this, scarse one word the wiser.[15]

Some few pulpits had traditions of their own which conditioned the delivery of sermons preached from them. Paul's Cross was the most important pulpit in England from which to deliver a sermon. Originally there had been no service there, and the sermons were preached with neither prologue nor epilogue. The returning Marian exiles, however, brought with them the continental custom of congregational singing and by 1560 there was regular singing of Psalms at the Cross at sermon time. Later prayers came to be added to the end of the sermon. Cambridge men were bound to

---

14. Manningham, *Diary*, p. 101.
15. *Ibid.*, p. 75.

pray for their chancellor when they preached and they usually included the Queen lest she feel slighted. When Dr. Dawson of Trinity, Cambridge, preached at Paul's Cross on November 14, 1602, "All the while he prayed he kept on his velvet night cap untill he came to name the Queene, and then of went that to, when he had spoken before both of and to God with it on his head."[16] Since one group of preachers used prayers at the Cross, others soon followed their example until the practice became standard.

To be asked to preach at court before Elizabeth was a high honor, but it partook somewhat of the nature of an ordeal as well. Elizabeth's knowledge of theology was nothing prodigious and neither was her interest in it, but she was extremely critical none the less. To speak freely before her was to displease her, for one of her few consistencies was her hatred of liberty of speech, especially if the speech concerned her. To speak with great reserve was to displease her also; she put the worst possible construction on all subtleties and she perceived threats in all dark passages. Not only was the preacher unable to compose a sermon certain to please her because of her shifting stand on theological matters, but his reception could not be guaranteed by the Queen's friendship, any previous graciousness, or even her expression of approval of men whom she had heard before. The preacher would be received graciously, apathetically, or icily, depending only upon the degree of charity of which the Queen happened to be possessed at the moment.

During the sermon Elizabeth sat in a private closet at a window facing the preacher. If she were displeased with the sermon she would close the shutters or retire to the inner recesses of the box unless she thought stronger measures warranted. If a man preached too long, Elizabeth would simply tell him to stop, or if he wandered into forbidden ground she might call him down on the spot. Once when Dean Nowell was preaching to her he left the main topic of his sermon and began to inveigh against images, but unfortunately it happened to be one of the days when the Queen liked images and so she pulled him up abruptly by shout-

16. *Ibid.*, p. 84.

ing to him to stick to his text, which the good dean thereafter did.[17]

Some preachers were exceeding brave men who preached to her without regard to her wishes. Bishop Westphaling, a man noted for his unshakable composure, while preaching an inordinately long sermon before Elizabeth twice refused to stop in the course of it when Her weary Majesty sent him orders by messenger to bring it to a close. When he had come to the end of what he had prepared he stopped, but not before.[18] Brave Archbishop Hutton, perhaps at the instigation of Parliament, preached to Elizabeth the necessity of choosing her successor — a very dangerous thing to do since she never allowed any discussion of the unpalatable fact that even queens grow old and die. The Queen in this instance was disturbed by the sermon and showed signs of resentment, but surprised everybody by thanking the preacher when he had finished. That she did not dismiss the insolence from her mind, however, can be seen from her attempts to procure a written copy of the sermon. In these she was unsuccessful, for Hutton well knew how expert Elizabeth was at misinterpretation if she wished to be, and so all she got from him was profuse excuses.[19] Another preacher dared to preach on the unsavory topic of death and was barely tolerated for it.

> Dr. Rud made a sermon before the Queene upon the text, "I sayd yee are Gods, but you shall all dy like men;" wherein he made such a discourse of death that hir Majestie, when his sermon was ended, said unto him, "Mr. Dr. you have made me a good funerall sermon, I may dye when I will."[20]

To please Elizabeth with a sermon was so difficult an achievement that preachers were not reluctant to see a successful court sermon go to press, as can be seen by the profusion of such sermons in the bibliography, where they bulk, perhaps, disproportionately large.[21]

---

17. Wood, *Athenae Oxonienses,* vol. I, column 717.
18. Harington, *Brief View,* quoted by F. O. White, *Lives of the Elizabethan Bishops,* p. 293.
19. *Ibid.,* pp. 305-7.
20. Manningham, *Diary,* p. 136.
21. Court sermons will be found in the bibliography under the following names or titles: H. B., Babington, Barlow, Cole, Curteys, Dering, Drant, Fulke, Humphrey, James, Jewel, *Peters Fall,* Rudd, L. S., *A Godlye Sermon, A Sermon Preached Before the Queenes Majestie,* Wentworth, Whitgift, and Young.

While some audiences were difficult to please and others quite unruly, the delivery of a sermon was at times as unseemly as the behavior in the nave. At St. Mary's, Oxford, in the beginning of Elizabeth's reign, to show that he was not a common clergyman but the high sheriff of the county of Oxford, Richard Taverner went into the pulpit wearing the gold chain of his office and even a sword as well as his ecclesiastical vestments.[22] At Buckland, William Holcot preached in a garb calculated to impress upon the audience the fact that he was a gentleman as well as a servant of the Church: he wore a rich damask gown, a gold chain, and, to top off this unusual apparel, a velvet bonnet.[23] The people liked such forbidden novelties in the pulpit, and the sermons of men sensational in either dress or sermon style were well attended. For pure outrage in the pulpit, however, no Elizabethan approached the actions and sermons of Hubberdin in the reign of Mary. Foxe, in his *Book of Martyrs,* tells of a sermon that attracted wide notice:

> Hubberdin . . . riding by a Church side where the Youth of the parish were dauncing in the Churchyard, sodainly this Silenus lighting from his horse, by the occasion of their dauncing came into the Church, and there causing the bell to toll in the people, thought in stead of a fit of mirth, to give them a sermon of dauncing. In the which Sermon after he had patched up certain common texts out of the Scriptures, and then comming to the doctors, first to Augustine, then to Ambrose, so to Hierome, and Gregory, Chrysostome, and other doctors, had made them every one to sing after his tune for the probation of the sacrament of the altar against John Frith, Zuinglius, Decolampadius, Luther, Tindall, Latimer, and other hereticks (as he called them) at last to shew a perfect harmony of all these doctors togither, as he had made them before to sing after his tune, so now to make them dance after his pipe, first he calleth out Christ and his Apostles, then the Doctors and ancient Seniours of the Church, as in a round ring all to daunce togither: with pipe up Hubberdin. Now daunce Christ, now daunce Peter, Paul, now daunce Augustine, Ambrose, Hierom: and thus old Hubberdin as he was dauncing with his Doctours lustilie in the pulpit, against the Hereticks, how he stampt and tooke on I cannot tell, but crash quoth the Pulpit, downe commeth the dancer, and there lay Hubberdin not dancing, but sprawling in the middest of his audience: where altogether he

22. Wood, *op. cit.*, vol. I, column 420.
23. *Ibid.*, vol. I, columns 395 and 420.

brake not his necke, yet hee so brake his legge the same time and bruised his old boanes, that he never came in Pulpit more, and dyed not long after the same.[24]

But just as the antics of some of our contemporary pseudo-divines are not typical of the conduct and dress of present day clergy, so these strange happenings in the pulpit of the sixteenth century were not typical of the clergy then; they merely illustrate to what extremes sensationalists could go. The average sermon was probably delivered as solemnly and certainly at greater length than most today. Except for the time when Bishop Parker climbed a tree at Norfolk to preach, the majority of the bishops behaved themselves "mighty mannerly" in the pulpit, and the lower clergy, on the whole, followed their example as best they could.

---

24. Foxe, *Actes and Monuments* (*Book of Martyrs*), edition of 1610, pp. 1581-2. Harington's epigram *Of Master John Davies Booke of Dancing* (book II, No. 67) also tells of Hubberdin's pulpit crash.

# CHAPTER III

## THE OCCASIONAL SERMON

*Preach the word, be instant in season.*

St. Paul

In the reign of Elizabeth no occasion of any magnitude at all was deemed properly observed or celebrated unless a sermon was preached, and the occasions of preaching were not ecclesiastical red letter days or emergencies only, but civil and social functions as well. When an observance was planned, a preacher was appointed in advance so that he might have sufficient time to prepare a sermon pertinent to the occasion. Such appointments were honors for the clergymen selected.

At ecclesiastical gatherings a sermon was of course expected. Whenever there was a convocation of the bishops or other dignitaries of the church to iron out difficulties in doctrine or church government, the meeting usually began by a preaching, often in Latin, by one of the hierarchy, and not infrequently the preaching was continued daily to open each session. To be asked to preach before so great and so learned an assembly was a mark of approval and also a chance to be cunning in subtle points of theology and to prove one's ability to preach in Latin. To preach well and soundly before convocation was a great stride towards preferment.[1]

Preaching was also a feature of the visitations of the dioceses

1. Sermons before convocation and other clerical sermons will be found in the bibliography under the names Bankes, Holland, Playfere, and Whitaker.

when the bishops or other appointed visitors in their steads made the rounds of important churches to take stock of virtue and to smell out any heresies they could. Sermons were delivered to the clergy and laity by the eminent visitors, and generally there were also sermons for the clergy only at which the presence of laity would have proved embarrassing.[2]

The public baptising of a Jew in 1578 called for a sermon; the baptising of a Turk at St. Katherine's Hospital in 1586 was even more of an event and Dr. Hanmer did both the baptising and the subsequent preaching.[3] At the other ecclesiastical extreme, an excommunication also demanded a sermon. When, in 1560, Bishop Bonner was excommunicated, the decree was not only the subject of a sermon at Paul's Cross, but was contained in the body of that sermon.

Another occasion that always brought forth a large number of sermons was the cessation of a violent epidemic of the plague.[4] While the importance of this was chiefly social, the clergy saw a religious significance behind it. While the plague raged, sermons to large audiences were not preached, since church services other than small gatherings to hear the plague litany and collects were wisely prohibited, together with performances in the theaters and other public gatherings, but when regular church services were allowed again, there were always sermons proving the plague to be a visitation of God, a fatherly chastisement to be profited of by all members of the Church. The end of the 1563/4 epidemic of the plague was celebrated in this manner:

> Anno 1564 . . . on ye Wedynsdaye, beynge ye 26 of Januarie, wasse a solome sermon made at Powlls Crosse by Coale, Archedecon of Essyxe, wherunto was warnyd ye Lord Mayre of London with ye Aldarmen and Shrives, with allso the crafftis of ye citie in theyr lyveries. Wher in ye prechar dyd move ye awdyence to rejoyce that ye plage wasse cleane sessyd, and that God had cleane takyn it awaye from us. He sayd ye cawsse ther of was ye superstysyows relygyon of Rome, whiche was (as he sayd) so myche favoryd of ye sytysyns. . . . and sayd

2. Visitation sermons will be found under the names Beatniffe, Godwin, and Overton.

3. These two sermons will be found under the names of their preachers, John Fox and Meredith Hanmer.

4. A number of plague sermons will be found in the bibliography by William Cupper, Richard Leake, and Thomas White.

that yf we dyd not beware of falce relygyon, all thowght God had cleane takyn a way y^e plage, he wold send a worse apon use, that is to say, fyre and sword, which shuld slee y^e children at ther mothars brestes, y^e wyffes shuld be slayn from theyr husbonds, y^e husbonds from theyr wyffes, and one neyghbour shuld sleye an othar to have his goods.[5]

The opening of a session of court regularly called for a sermon to be delivered to the judges, noblemen, gentry, and people assembled. These sermons, as might be expected, were mostly conventional exhortations to truth, justice, and mercy, and to the punishment of wickedness and vice, calculated to open no controversial issue, and to offend nobody except the wicked and vicious. Several assize and other court sermons were printed and will be found in the bibliography.[6]

The opening of Parliament was the occasion of a sermon. The Queen, attended by the lords and bishops, rode in state from the palace to the Abbey Church of St. Peter, where the entire company listened to a sermon and sang a psalm or two before the actual ceremonies of the opening of the Parliament across the road.

The anniversary of the Queen's accession, which fell on November 17, was another day celebrated by preaching, among other things more worldly. That Elizabeth should be the subject of a sermon was appropriate enough since she was the head of the Church. The day was hailed by the clergy as a fine excuse publicly and loudly to pledge allegiance to Elizabeth and to pile the compliments to the toppling point; it was patent that the Queen advanced only men of known allegiance to the higher offices of the Church. Men who were known as trouble-makers or who were out of favor at the moment took advantage of the day to placate the Crown, while others also preached from reasonable motives of true admiration or patriotism. A relatively large proportion of these Queen's Day sermons found their way to the press.[7]

Most of the occasions mentioned occurred annually or at least repeatedly, and so a tradition of preaching grew up around the observances. But there was something more behind these ser-

5. Stow, *Memoranda,* p. 128.
6. For assize sermons see the bibliography under the names Hutchins, Kethe, Overton, Miles Smith, and Westerman.
7. Queen's Day sermons will be found under these names: Colfe, Harris, Holland, Howson, Prime, and Thos. White.

mons than the mere following of tradition, and this can be seen by the fact that unexpected and unprecedented occasions brought forth sermons just as surely and abundantly.

The fire at St. Paul's Cathedral in 1561 was just the type of thing to inspire sermons. Lightning struck a bell tower, fired the cathedral, and melted the bells. Upon one thing only was everybody agreed, that the storm and lightning and the consequent fires were acts of God and open to interpretation. Bishop Pilkington, both able and willing to preach, used the catastrophe as his text the following Sunday and held it to be a warning to remove a few remaining abuses from the Church of England. As for the cathedral's purity in the days of Roman administration he had much to say:

> No place had been more abused than Paul's had been, nor more against the receiving of Christ's gospel: wherefore it was more marvel, that God spared it so long, than that he overthrew it now. . . . The south alley was for usury and popery; the north for simony; and the horse-fair in the midst for all kind of bargains, meetings, brawlings, murders, conspiracies. The font for ordinary payments of money, as well known to all men, as the beggar knows his dish. . . . So that without and within, above the ground and under, over the roof and beneath, on the top of the steeple and spire, down to the low floor, not one spot was free from wickedness. . . . God's house must be a house of prayer, and not the proud tower of Babylon, nor the pope's market-place, nor a stews for bawds and ruffians, nor a horse-fair for brokers; no, nor yet a burse for merchants, nor a meeting-place for walking and talking.[8]

From other sources, however, it is clear that the use of the cathedral as a social and commercial center continued as lustily under Elizabeth as under Mary, and the Romanists were well aware of this. Unable to preach openly to confute Pilkington, they employed rumor to state that the fire and storm were a sign of God's displeasure at the forsaking of Holy Mass in the cathedral and at the corporate heresy of the Church of England. One Roman protest against Pilkington's sermon admitted some of the earlier abuses of the cathedral, but continued in this vein:

> Although these [abuses] be very evil and worthy much rebuke, yet there be worse abuses, as blaspheming God in lying sermons, polluting the temple with schismatical service, destroying and pulling down holy altars, that were set up by good blessed men, and there the sacrifice of the blessed mass ministered ac-

8. Strype, *Annals,* vol. I, pt. 1, pp. 391-2.

cording to the order of Christs catholic church. Yea, where the altar stood of the Holy Ghost, the new bishops have made a place to set their tails upon, and there sit in judgment of such as be catholic and live in the fear of God.[9]

Again the next Sunday Dean Nowell, preaching at Paul's Cross, used the adjacent burned cathedral as his subject, and the sermon was largely a request that the rebuilding be speedy. Another sermon was evoked from the Bishop of London on November 1, the same year, when the cathedral was again opened for services. This first service in the newly reopened church was a very festive occasion and was attended in state by the Lord Mayor and the Aldermen in their robes of office.

When unbridled Protestantism ran amok, fine stained glass windows were smashed, roodbeams and the figures thereon were pulled down and burned together with countless books, altars were desecrated, and fine churches were irreparably ruined. This vandalism was accompanied by sermons of approval.[10] These outrages were not to the level-headed Queen's taste, to be sure, but they had the sanction of certain fanatical local clergy who as they preached by the light of the burning art treasures did not yet understand the unswerving determination of Elizabeth that the wolves of Geneva as well as the long arm of Rome were to be kept out of England. They were yet to discover that the forensic power that could produce the sermons could not dissuade the Queen from vengeance. Disinterested agents of the Crown calculated the damage and noted it down, and the damages were assessed against the parishes.[11] It behooved these fire-light preachers, if they had wit enough to see their error, to preach loudly and soundly on the next November 17.

A national crisis like the coming of the Spanish Armada would occasion sermons of a patriotic nature all over England. When patriotic themes were exhausted, standard and superlative attacks upon Rome and vilification of the papal powers behind Spain were in order. We find that even a small local "trayning of souldiers"

9. Possibly by John Moren or Morwen, chaplain to Bishop Bonner. Printed in *Works of James Pilkington*, p. 483.
10. Cf. Strype, *Annals*, vol. I, pt. 1, p. 254.
11. Cf. Royal Proclamation of September 19, 1559.

was the occasion of a sermon preached by Edmond Harris at the estate of Sir John Brocket.[12]

A private crisis like a wedding could also bring forth a sermon.[13] To be sure, a wedding of lesser folk needed no more sermon than present-day nuptials, but a marriage between members of the nobility or near-nobility that would attract a large gathering of important persons was felt to require a sermon, preferably by a prelate or other church dignitary. Lady Huntington thus asked the Dean of York to preach:

> After my verye hartie commendacions. Forasmuch as a kinsman of my lorde and a cosen of myne doe intend, by the grace of God, to marrye together uppon Sondaye nexte, I am therefore bould to desyre you, that you would take the paynes to be here againste that tyme, and to bestowe a shorte sermon uppon us, suche as for the short warning you have maye suffise for that audience. The which ended, or before, att your discretion, I muste further intreate you to helpe to sollempnize that marriage. And even soe, being bould to truble you, I doe bidd you hartelye fare well. Att York, this xxj^th of Julye, 1575.[14]

One more occasion that sometimes required a sermon was a funeral. While there had been sermons at funerals before this time, they were infrequent, and preaching at funerals of ordinary common people was an innovation in the beginning of Elizabeth's reign. Before this, there had been Requiem Mass and a ceremonial interment, together with a choral procession to the grave. Now a funeral consisted of a silent procession to the grave, a few psalms, a lesson, the interment with the casting of dirt; then the party adjourned to the church and heard a sermon. This service was not unlike the present burial service of the Church of England, save that the sermon is not now required. The bigger and more important the funeral, the more the care that was given to the sermon. The most celebrated funerals of the time were the corpseless funerals of foreign rulers; it was a matter of international courtesy thus to observe the death of a head of a friendly power. These were very elaborate services and were attended by high ranking officials and nobles. The first of these that fell in the reign of Elizabeth was the funeral of Henry II of France. After great preparation, decoration, and distribution of mourning gar-

12. *A Sermon preached at Brocket Hall,* 1588.
13. Wedding sermons by Henry Smith and Wm. Massie were printed.
14. Hutton, *Correspondence,* letter IV.

ments, which cost Elizabeth the tidy sum of £789/10/10, the funeral was solemnly celebrated on the afternoon of September 8, 1559, and the next morning. The sermon was preached on the morning of the second day by Bishop-elect Scory of Hereford, the Bishop of London being ill. This sermon was hardly what was expected at so great a funeral, for after proving that the Day of Doom was then at hand, the bishop spent most of his time inveighing against the stupidity and pointlessness of elaborate funerals. The Communion that followed was no more successful than the sermon. Since a Requiem Mass could not be sung, the new Communion Service was used, and that without any prayers for the departed. To the foreign delegation the new service was strange and unpalatable, and to most of the native nobility present it was not pleasing either, with the result that only three of the nobility and three of the presiding clergy went up to receive the elements after the new and, to the minds of the gentry present, blasphemous fashion.[15]

Other and more successful funerals for foreign monarchs were held in St. Paul's. Archbishop Sandys preached at the state funeral of Charles IX of France and tactfully neglected to mention imbecility, and Bishop Grindal of London preached at the funeral of the Emperor Ferdinand. These grand funerals were few in number, but they undoubtedly helped to set a precedent for the growing custom of having a sermon preached at even the most lowly funeral. A great many sermons preached at the funerals of English gentry were printed and will be found in the bibliography.[16]

---

15. Strype, *Annals*, vol. I, pt. 1, pp. 187-91.

16. Funeral sermons in the bibliography will be found under these names: Anderson, Babington, Chamberlaine, Davies, Grindal, Leygh, Harrison, Hooker, Sparke, and White. Bishop Grindal's sermon was also printed in a Latin version for foreign readers.

# CHAPTER IV

## OFFICIAL INSPIRATION OF SERMONS

*What ye hear in the ear, that preach.*

St. Matthew

In addition to sermons preached in season and out of season as prescribed by St. Paul, and sermons preached quarterly according to the injunctions of the Queen, certain other sermons were preached by particular request of authorities both ecclesiastical and civil. The matter to be treated, and in a few cases even the manner of treatment, was officially inspired. Detailed evidence of such inspiration is, however, rare, as might be expected, since the force of the sermon on the audience would be lost if it were known that pressure had been put upon the preacher.

It is not surprising to find that ecclesiastical inspiration is more common and less interesting than civil inspiration. The sermon of Bernard Gilpin would be an example of inspiration coming from officials of the Church. During a visitation to the northern dioceses in the year 1559 for the purpose of administering the Oath of Supremacy required of all clergy, Gilpin, a Catholic-minded rector, was given a most unpleasant assignment by the visiting ecclesiastical authorities.

These visitors of the northern parts came to Aukland; where they sent for the clergy of that diocese to appear before them; and among other things gave them a declaration to subscribe. Dr. Sandys, one of the visitors, preached. They sent to Bernard Gilpin, of the bishopric of Durham, and required him to preach at Durham; and gave him his subject, which was against the *primacy* [of the pope]. Because the oath of supremacy being to be required of all the clergy, they might be the better prepared to take it.[1]

Gilpin was so upset by Sandys' very Protestant sermon against the Real Presence and by his own sermon subject that he could not sleep, and had grave doubts whether he could subscribe to the oath himself; but he did preach the sermon required of him. Having reasoned that stirring up strife within the Church by refusing was worse than his own doubts, he did not preach hypocritically. His example in approving the oath by both word and deed had just the effect that had been calculated by the assigners of the sermon; the clergy took the oath acknowledging Elizabeth as the head of the Church and peace reigned in Durham. The end of the visitation, however, was marred by a death. Gilpin's curate, in whose craw the oath also stuck, died when he had signed the oath and it was a matter of discussion whether he had been struck down by God for his hypocrisy or whether acute alcoholic poisoning had merely claimed another victim.[2] Ignoring this delicate question, the visitors moved on.

When men preached to religious offenders in prison by official assignment, as happened rather frequently, there was less need to hide the fact that they preached by order of authority.[3] Such information is even given on title pages of printed sermons. When John Keltridge in 1581 preached two sermons to the Jesuits imprisoned in the Tower "in which were confuted to their faces, the moste principall and cheefe poincts of their Romish and Whoarish religion: and all such Articles as they defend, contrarie to the woord of God, were layed open and ripped up unto them", the title page of these sermons announces that they were "appointed."

From the zest with which Keltridge discharged his duties it may be assumed that the assignment caused him none of the conscientious scruples that worried Bernard Gilpin, but neither did it cause any great conversion of the bepreached Jesuits. The

1. Strype, *Annals*, vol. I, pt. 1, p. 246.

2. Strype, *Annals*, vol. I, pt. 1, p. 247. "This gave occasion to some disaffected, to suppose that his subscription had killed him. But others said, that his sickness proceeded from excessive drinking."

3. Assigned Tower sermons preached by Dering, Fulke, and Keltridge were printed and will be found in the bibliography.

preacher remarked on the poor reception of this type of inspired sermon:

I did finde, that the travaile and study of theirs [the appointed preachers] hath to this day taken so small effect, as not onely the Jesuites are more and more stiffned in their errors; But also, they are become so sencelese in feeling, so blunt in attayning, so wicked and malicious in resisting, so disloyall and spitefull in hearing, so sturdie and malaperte in withstanding openlie the teachers of the Gospell; as the people are upon the same dismayed, zealous and godly men discouraged, and all sortes of people moste pittifully distracted, that either heere or see them at any time.[4]

Today we are not so much surprised at the Jesuits' response as we are at Mr. Keltridge's hopes, and doubt not that the Jesuits were the most pitifully distracted of the people there.

While civil inspiration is more interesting than ecclesiastical inspiration, it is also more difficult to prove. It is certain that the state constantly used the larger pulpits, such as Paul's Cross, for the dissemination of propaganda.[5] To civil authorities preachers would apply for official news, and might even ask whether they could be of any other service while they were in the pulpit. Such a letter is that of Bishop Grindal to Cecil:

I pray you let me understand, whether it may be certainly avouched that the king of Navarre, the second Julian, is killed. I intend (God willing) to preach at the cross the next Sunday, and upon occasion offered would peradventure make some mention of God's judgments over him, if the same be true and certain; else not. If there be any other matter which ye wish to be uttered there for the present state, I would be pleased to know it in time, if your leisure will serve. God keep you![6]

There is one complete record of the civil inspiration of a sermon for the purpose of disseminating important official propaganda, and this is found in letters and other documents dealing with the rebellion and subsequent execution of Essex. The colorful and charming earl was exceedingly popular, and to shift public sentiment around to supporting the Crown's case against him it was deemed wise to spread the propaganda from the pulpit since this

---

4. *Two Sermons in the Tower,* sig. *2.

5. Civil inspiration of important sermons was not an innovation of Elizabeth's reign. In 1549 King Edward sent Bishop Bonner notes from which he was ordered to preach his first sermon at St. Paul's. He ignored the notes and was sent to prison as a consequence. See *C.S.P.D. Edward VI,* vol. VIII, No. 36 and No. 57.

6. October 28, 1562. Grindal, *Remains,* p. 253.

was the quickest medium for reaching the people.[7] We have a contemporary letter telling of the Star Chamber's resolution just before the trial of Essex:

> Order was taken the Sunday following that the preachers at Paul's cross and other churches in London should deliver the same matters from the pulpit, and decry the Earl as a hypocrite, Papist, and confederate with the Pope and King of Spain, to make him King and bring in idolatry. But as is usual in such cases, they, from malice or desire to please, amplified it beyond all probability. On the one side they cry "Crucify;" on the other there is such a jealousy of light and bad fellows, that it is rumoured the preachers of London will rise and deliver him out of the Tower.[8]

The effect of such indiscriminate and widespread preaching was obviously not at all what was desired, and another time things were ordered differently. The prosecution, however, had learned something from the reaction of the people and modified its charges against the earl accordingly. John Chamberlain noted this and pointed it out to his correspondent:

> I must needes say that one thing sticks much in many mens minde that whereas divers preachers were commaunded the Sonday before to deliver to the people among his other treasons that he had complotted with Tirone, and was reconciled to the Pope; and whereas Master Atturny at Tom Leas arraignment, averred the same combining with Tiron, and that he had practised by the meanes of seminarie preists with the Pope and the king of Spaine to be king of England: there was no such matter once mentioned at his arraignment, and yet there was time enough for yt, from nine aclocke in the morning till almost seven at night.[9]

When the trial was over and Essex duly executed, popular opinion was still not satisfactory and again the civil authorities turned to the pulpit. But this time, instead of inciting all sorts of irresponsible clergy to distort the propaganda from a hundred pulpits, they resolved to have but one sermon preached and that to the huge audience at Paul's Cross by Dr. Barlow, a man particularly fitted to do this by virtue of the fact that it was he who attended Essex in his last hours. Accordingly, Secretary Cecil wrote to Dr. Barlow and gave him minute instructions as to the

---

7. The official *Directions for the Preachers* is printed in *C.S.P.D. Elizabeth,* vol. CCLXXVIII, No. 63.

8. From a letter by Vincent Hussey printed in *C.S.P.D. Elizabeth,* vol. CCLXXVIII, No. 94.

9. *Letters,* I, 120.

contents of the sermon he was commanded to preach, and happily this letter is preserved.

> I leave all the things which I have delivered you by my Lords' direction to be carried and applied as you like, only the Lords desire that when you touch the practice and purpose of coming to Court with a power, you move them to consider how perilous a thing it was to have put a lady, a Queen, in that fright she must have been in; for when it was appointed that Sir Christ. Blount with one company should seize the gate, another company should possess the hall with Sir John Davies, and a third should master the guard by seizing the halberts in the guard chamber, and Sir Ch. Danvers master the presence chamber with another company, how can it be imagined but some resistance would be made? Blood once drawn, more would have followed, which would have been no small horror to the Queen's nature. Neither can it be expected that these three commanders, Blount, Davies, and Ch. Danvers, whereof the first two are proved to be Papists, and the third that way affected, would have cared much to commit any insolence rather than be frustrated in their designs. That this was true the Earl penitently confessed, also the Earl of Southampton, Sir Ch. Danvers, Sir John Davies, and Sir Ferd. Gorges (all men yet untried), confess it.
>
> Yet the Earl ever protested that when he entered into the purpose, and sent the articles to be considered of at Drury House, he ever resolved to have all things done with as little blood as could be; and for the Queen's own person, would never have suffered it to receive any harm.
>
> In anywise remember to name the particulars of his obstinate speeches to Mr. Dove, which my Lord of London can deliver you. Remember also precisely to declare it, so as it may be clearly conceived how great suit the Earl made that he might die privately in the Tower, and how much he even to yourself expressed his thankfulness for it, wherein also you may not forget how himself was possessed with an opinion that he should have had of the people a great acclamation. If you can bring it in well, it will be very fit to remember that his purpose of taking the Tower was only to have been a bridle to the city, if happily the city should have misliked his other attempt.[10]

Dr. Barlow followed the directions and preached a sermon the next Sunday which was presumably satisfactory to the authorities.[11] The audience, however, was aware that this was a strange sort of sermon and all kinds of rumors sprang up about both the sermon and the preacher. Dr. Barlow can best tell the aftermath of this sermon himself:

> I confesse, that the addressing my selfe to this sermon (containing in it matter rather of state then divinitie, and beeing like unto the preamble of the Pharisees in my text, 'αμφιχρηνός, subject to offence one way, eyther to them

10. *C.S.P.D. Elizabeth,* vol. CCLXXVIII, No. 126.
11. *A Sermon preached at Paules Crosse,* 1601.

of authoritie if I should renounce this dutie, or the auditorie if I should speake of uncertaintie) was as the Apostle speaketh, 'εν φõϐω και πὸμω, with much feare and trembling. . . . Notwithstanding all this my care and paines, the malignitie of the meany is such, that, as if I had either with Ananias lied unto the holy Ghost, and had preached mine own damnation, as it pleased some to blaspheme, it was given out that I was stroken, if not with madnesse, yet with dreadfull sicknesse; or, as if I had spoken treason, that I was, the next day, committed close prisoner to the Tower; or at least, I had highly offended her majestie, and received great check from the Councell. The two first my body can answere, which hath beene, I thanke God, ever sithence, in latitudine sanitatis et libertatis, both in health, and at libertie; the two last cannot be throughly confuted by me, without some opinion of vanity and selfe glory, unlesse that be checking, which Euripides calleth 'ευφημα φωνειν honourable words, above my desertes.[12]

Certainly there is not so complete a record of any other officially inspired sermon of the period, but doubtless there were many more which, not being connected with anything so sensational as the execution of Essex, were arranged with more secrecy and have left no evidence behind them. Even the search for evidence of official inspiration of sermons relating to the execution and several funerals of Mary Queen of Scots has been fruitless. There are records of the sermons and comments on them, but if they were inspired, as it is reasonable to suppose they were, the authorities used more finesse than in the Essex case.

12. *Op. cit.*, sig. A2 recto.

# CHAPTER V

## CONTROVERSIAL SERMONS

*Now did both the evangelics and the papalins bestir themselves.*

JOHN STRYPE

Sermons on subjects engendering theological controversy were strictly forbidden both by the Queen and the prelates. Elizabeth's point in prohibiting them was doubtless the preservation of the peace and not any great fear of the spread of theories or doctrines repugnant to her. The fine points of religion were of little importance to her one way or the other, but contention over these matters she would not abide.

Archbishop Parker had ordered the clergy to "abstain from busy meddling with matters of controversy"[1] because he saw that the contentions were invariably profitless. Nothing was ever gained by the wrangling except more fissures in the none too strong wall of the Church. The new position of the Church of England, neatly balanced between Protestantism and Catholicism, was difficult enough to maintain without confusion and dissension within, and so the bishops had grounds enough to forbid disturbing discussions. Archbishop Whitgift viewed controversial sermons in this light:

For what is it to preach every day, and to spend the time with words only, or with bitter invectives against certain trifles, and against superiors? Such sermons do not edify, but destroy, do not work in the hearts of the hearers faith and charity, but either contempt of religion, or else contempt of superiors,

1. Strype, *Annals,* vol. I, pt. 1, p. 329.

contempt of good orders, yea, hatred, malice, undiscreet wrath coloured with a pretence of zeal. Truly such sermons seldom or never work any good effect: many women in London could on that sort occupy the time.[2]

None the less, in spite of the interdicts, a great many controversial sermons were preached, and not only preached but printed as well. These printed sermons, however, do not reflect the great religious controversies of the day save in a few exceptions. To preach on a trifling controversy would arouse only trifling notice, but preachers hesitated to launch into a vital controversial point because of the unwelcome amount of attention such a proceeding would attract. Ecclesiastical superiors would not only hear of vital controversial sermons, but probably get garbled versions of them which would make explanations difficult and dangerous.

Another reason why sermons on disputed doctrines and usages do not bulk larger in the printed sermon literature is that, besides being dangerous to preach, they were almost impossible to print. If the printing of a controversial sermon was contemplated, the preacher had to consider not only his ecclesiastical superiors, but theoretically the civil government as well. Officers of the crown could act in the case of the printed sermon since all material for publication had to pass a fairly rigid censorship which could be exercised by the Queen, members of the privy council, and the Archbishop of Canterbury. Actually, however, this civil censorship was really ecclesiastical, for in practice licenses for publication were granted by licensers appointed by the archbishop only. Unsavory controversial sermons would by this means be prohibited by the Church in the name of the civil government, and publication without a license became a felony incurring rigorous punishment. Therefore in the face of ecclesiastical surveillance and the threat of civil punishment it is not strange that the major religious controversies are not represented among the printed sermons in numbers proportionate to their importance.

Besides the arguing of dangerous and disputed matters of religious doctrine, the interdicts forbade discussion of affairs of state. Indeed, a preacher's meddling in matters of state or the Queen's private business was probably the most heinous offense of

---

2. *Defence of the Answer to the Admonition,* tractate XI, section 1.

all. John Chamberlain tells of a trespass by Bishop Babington on a very sore subject:

> The earle of Essex hath ben lately troubled with his old disease of loosenes, but yet tarries still by yt where he was, as a man quite out of minde: and yet Babington bishop of Worcester preaching at Court on Sonday last, made many profers and glaunces in his behalfe, as he was understoode by the whole auditorie, and by the Quene herself, who presently calling him to a reckening for yt, he flatly forswore that he had any such meaninge.[3]

Political and religious contentions were discussed in the pulpits, however, because it came to be understood that there were certain exceptions to the inhibitions against controversial preaching. If you could be very sure just where the Queen stood on a controversial matter, you could probably preach with impunity on the Queen's side. The Roman Catholic Church, for instance, was a safe subject for a sermon provided that you attacked it for being Roman and not for being Catholic; no person could (or can) tell whether Elizabeth was Protestant or Catholic, but it was patent that she would have none of the Bishop of Rome's claims to power, either spiritual or temporal, outside of the diocese of Rome. That there could be no doubt about this, Parliament in 1563 passed "An act for the assurance of the queen's royal power over all states and subjects in her dominions" in which penalties were provided for any person who

> shall by Writing, Cyphering, Printing, Preaching or Teaching, deed or Act, advisedly and wittingly hold or stand with, to extol, set forth, maintain or defend the Authority, Jurisdiction or Power of the Bishop of Rome, or of his See, heretofore claimed, used or usurped within this Realm.[4]

Thus secure in knowledge of the Queen's stand, when the Pope dethroned Elizabeth in 1570 Bishop Jewel did not hesitate to denounce Pope Pius V in as hot words as he could summon up.[5] Time to hesitate or to think up hotter words he did not have, for the infuriating bull was delivered to him while he was already in the pulpit preaching, and after a reading of it he preached a confutation extempore. Of course, no one could protest against this meddling in a major religious controversy because the very throne of England had been attacked. On the Good Friday following

---

3. *Letters,* I, 92-3.
4. *Statutes,* Anno Quinto Reg. Eliz., cap. 1.
5. *A view of a seditious Bul sent into England.*

Jewel's sermon John Fox the martyrologist mounted the pulpit at Paul's Cross and preached another blast at the Roman Church which also was motivated by the papal bull.[6] After these two major controversial sermons had been preached with impunity it became apparent that the Roman Church could be attacked by any preacher to his heart's content and that he would not be reproved; attacks became almost a patriotic duty. The number of anti-Roman sermons that followed and continued beyond Elizabeth's reign is huge; preachers all over England looked into the book of *Revelation* and found fine lurid texts which would stir the most apathetic congregation to attention and which would provide the preacher with starting points for vilification of any degree of outrageousness.[7]

William Fulke in 1570 preached a significant sermon[8] in which he proved to his own and to his auditors' satisfaction that the Babylon mentioned in *Revelation* is none other than Rome, and that Rome, like Babylon, is fallen. His text on this occasion immediately became an extremely popular one: "She is fallen, she is fallen, even Babylon that great Citie, for the wyne of the fury of her fornication she hath made all nations to drink."[9] The groundwork of this sermon was most ingenious, for Fulke had taken into consideration the people's delight in the mysteries of numerology. Starting with the Beast who figures prominently in *Revelation* as the sum of all the evil in the world, the preacher sought to link this further title of "the beast" to the Pope as well as that of "the great whore of Babylon". A verse in *Revelation* gave him the necessary starting point: "Here is wisdom. Let him that hath understanding count the number of the beast: for it is the number of a man; and his number is six hundred three-score and six."[10] Feeling that he had this understanding mentioned in the text, Fulke counted the number as instructed and also found the man whose number it was. The mechanics of this counting involved

6. *A Sermon of Christ Crucified,* 1570.

7. Chapters 14, 17, and 18 of *Revelation* especially.

8. *A Sermon preached at Hampton Court.*

9. Revelation 14:8. Another sermon on this theme will be found at the end of William Perkins' *Lectures upon the three first chapters of the Revelation.*

10. *Revelation* 13:18.

the Greek alphabet, numerological charts, and above all a great deal of ingenuity. He did it thus:

| | |
|---|---|
| λ | 30 |
| α | 1 |
| τ | 300 |
| ε | 5 |
| ι | 10 |
| ν | 50 |
| ο | 70 |
| ς | 200 |
| Λατεινος | 666 |

Who, then, could doubt that the Pope was the Beast?[11]

While sermons as sensational as this were undoubtedly delightful to the congregations, a great many of the more conservative clergy could not bring themselves to participate in such base mudslinging. These conservatives, however, soon found that they could preach against Rome and still maintain their dignity by either attacking doctrines or policies and not persons, or by assuming a superficially defensive attitude for the purpose of assault. A sermon delivered in the presence of the Queen by an unknown preacher is an example of a dignified attack; the office of the Pope is treated in an attempt to show that the broad powers of the office are unwarranted by scripture, while the Pope himself is not styled anything particularly offensive.[12] Again, Lawrence Humphrey, a returned Puritan exile, preached a course of seven sermons on the controversy with the Roman Church in which he also attempted to refrain from personalities and concentrated on the treasonable aspect of English subjects' membership in the Roman fold.[13] Assault in the disguise of defence more or less preserved dignity in the case of Bishop Cooper of Lincoln, who aimed a round dozen successive sermons at Roman doctrine and maintained that these sermons were "the defense of the Gospell nowe preached against such Cavils and false accusations, as are objected

11. *Op. cit.*, sig. B6 recto. The numerological basis of the computation and the method are not explained.
12. *A Godlye Sermon: Preached before the Queenes most excellent Majestie*, 1585 or before.
13. *A View of the Romish Hydra and Monster*, 1588.

both against the Doctrine it self, and the Preachers and Professors thereof, by the friendes and favourers of the Church of Rome."[14] A third means of keeping an attack dignified was to preach against heresy, for heresy has ever been a legitimate target for shafts from the pulpit. It was a master strategist and a bold who first thought of turning the tables and declaring the mother church to be heretical. John Dyos was not that strategist, for he was of too dull a mind, but we have a sermon by Dyos in which he belabors the Roman Catholic Church for heresy. Zeal, however, was Dyos' stumbling block, for he descended to calling names such as "malignant rable" and checked himself just in time from adding the amazing charge of schism to that of heresy.[15] This sermon, though not a prime example, suffices to show the possibilities of this plan of attack.

At the other extreme of important controversial matters stood the Puritans. The Church of England was not likely to censure attacks upon them, since one of their main planks was the abolition of episcopal government in the church, but they were not so easy to attack with impunity from the civil government because many persons in high places were known to have Puritan leanings, even if the Queen did not, and so the injunctions in this case were obeyed for a while. Then, too, at the first breaking away from Rome it had not appeared that Geneva would come to be an enemy of the Church of England also. But as the power of Rome waned, the menace of strict Protestantism became more evident. In February 1589 Dr. Bancroft steeled himself to the task and preached the first important sermon against the English Puritans and thus threw that controversial subject open to more preaching.[16] Bancroft had reason to expect that he might preach without censure if he played up the Puritans not only as schismatics, but as enemies to Elizabeth and the aristocracy. Therefore in attacking them he emphasized their disbelief in episcopal government of the church and made it plain that this disbelief came of

---

14. *Certaine Sermons,* 1580.

15. *A Sermon preached at Paules Crosse,* 1579.

16. *A Sermon preached at Paules Crosse,* 1589. One immediate result of this sermon was John Penry's treatise, *A brief discovery of the untruthes and slanders contained in a Sermon preached the 8. of Februarie 1588 by D. Bancroft.*

their grudging Elizabeth her first fruits, tenths, and other gifts that she demanded from men whom she appointed to church office. While condemning them for rejecting the *Book of Common Prayer* and the *Articles of Religion,* he made it clear that in rejecting article thirty-eight, which concerns private ownership of goods, they affirmed a belief in common ownership highly repugnant to the aristocracy. In this manner Dr. Bancroft got the Queen and the aristocracy on his side by his well chosen arguments, the prelates by championing episcopacy, and the common people by the superior oratory for which he was justly famous.

This precedent, however, did not guarantee impunity for other controversial sermons against strict Protestantism; others followed Bancroft into the field, but came out not unwounded. Though Cambridge was a seat of Calvinistic Protestantism and thus was at loggerheads with the Church of England, even here zealous anti-Genevans essayed to preach after Bancroft's example. In 1595 William Barret, a fellow of Caius College, attacked Calvin, both as a man and for his doctrines, in a Latin sermon to which exception was taken by the authorities. The wrangling over this incident did not end until Barret recanted after a conference with the archbishop at Lambeth. He was sent down from the university and in return for this treatment he became a Roman Catholic layman.[17] But Barret had no sooner left than Peter Baro, Lady Margaret professor of divinity, took his place as a disturber and in a sermon attacked Calvin's doctrine of predestination, a cornerstone of Protestantism, and also advocated a broader interpretation of the Atonement, which was held by Calvin to have been made only for those predestined to salvation and not for all men. Baro's objection was interpreted as Catholicism and so steps were taken to suppress it. In the course of the contention started by this sermon, the archbishops, the chancellor, and the heads of the colleges all disagreed. To secure peace a conference drew up certain articles to which it was proposed to require conformity. These, known as the Lambeth Articles, were quite Calvinistic in their acceptance of predestination. But all this

17. *C.S.P.D. Elizabeth,* vol. CCLII, No. 24, No. 67, and No. 78.

compromise to preserve the peace was in vain, for when Elizabeth saw the articles she promptly denounced them, probably as much because they had been drawn up without consulting her as because she really disagreed with the doctrine they contained. Seeing the attitude of the Queen, everybody from Robert Cecil through the archbishops to the university authorities hastily washed his hands of the articles, and Baro continued in office.[18] Unable to see a more clearly defined stand on Genevan Protestantism by either civil or ecclesiastical government, most preachers realized that the subject were better avoided in public utterances and in print.

For the reasons noted, then, the greater controversies do not figure prominently in the printed sermons. What the censors were willing to pass were mostly small attacks upon portions of the service or official doctrine, or sermons delivered in the course of private and personal contentions.

Edward Philips, being a reputable clergyman, was allowed to preach and print his dislike of the general confession.

> [A sinner] may not thinke to obtaine the comfort of Gods countenence by blurting out a short prayer, that passeth out of thy mouth like gunshot, as, Lord I have sinned.[19]

Edward Dering (although he was later inhibited from preaching) was also allowed to attack doctrines that were not essential; he devoted a sermon, for example, to the long cold controversy over the nature of angels and the nine orders thereof.[20] More likely to be forbidden was his sermon against the observation of saint's days and Lent, since the Church of England expected such observance.

> The true worshippers should not go to mount Sion nor to Jerusalem, but worship God in spirit & truth. Where said he, go a pilgrimage, or goe visit the holy sepulchre? God said: Doe not observe dayes, and moneths, and times, and yeeres. Where said he, keepe unto me, Lent or Advent, imber weekes, or Saincts Eeves? God said unto us: It is the doctrine of devils to forbid marriage, or to commaund to abstaine from meats. Where said hee, eate nowe no fleashe, now no whit meat: let not ye minister marrie?[21]

Publication of this lecture was not prohibited, but Dering was

---

18. Strype, *Whitgift,* II, 288 ff.
19. *Certaine godly and learned Sermons,* before 1605, sermon No. 8.
20. *XXVII Lectures on Hebrues,* 1576, lecture No. 6.
21. *Ibid.,* lecture No. 3.

restrained from further lecturing at St. Paul's.[22] Even an archbishop would touch upon minor controversial matter; the very Lent observances that Dering attacked were scoffed at by Archbishop Sandys in a sermon:

> Again, there is a superstitious humility, such as that was, "Touch not, taste not, handle not:" touch not the chalice, taste not an egg in Lent, handle not the bread that by consecration is made holy: which things had a shew of religious holiness, but were indeed mere dalliances, devised by Satan, to no other end, but only to noozle the deceived in their blindness.[23]

A minor controversy — and it must have been very minor since nobody would dare openly to take the other side — flared up over the celebration of the anniversary of Elizabeth's coronation. Whether the critics of the festivities were real or only straw men set up to motivate patriotic sermons we do not know, but Dr. Howson, chaplain to the Queen, preached a sermon "in defence of the Festivities of the Church of England, and namely that of her Majesties Coronation"[24] and Regius Professor Dr. Holland another "Whereby all such sclanderous Accusations are fully and faithfully confuted, whereby the Honour of the Realme hath beene uncharitably traduced by some of our adversaries in foraine nations, and at home, for observing the 17. of November yeerely in the form of an Holy-day, and for the joifull exercises, and the Courtly triumphes on that day in honour of her Majesty exhibited".[25] Since any person to openly refute sermons of this tenor would have to be out of his mind, these preachers must have carried the day.

So many were these sermons that treated of minor controversial matter that we even have a sermon inspired by their prevalence. Mr. Butler, Rector of Oundle, preached a sermon at Cambridge "succinctly debating the chiefe matters, which are now in question in the Church of England. Verie profitable for the further resolving of them, who being brought into suspence by the contradiction of Ministers, are content to lend an indifferent eare unto the truth."[26]

---

22. Strype, *Whitgift,* III, 34.
23. Sandys, *Works,* sermon No. 5, §13.
24. *A Sermon Preached at S. Maries,* 1602.
25. Πανηγυρις *D. Elizabethae,* 1599.
26. *A learned and notable Sermon,* 1593 or before.

It is important to see that out of these rather innocuous sermons in which men took exception to small portions of the official doctrine of the Established Church grew the more important and vitriolic private controversies. Private, in one sense, they were not, for they were carried on in the public pulpit and in printed books, but they were private in that they were very personal controversies and involved private animosities. These private controversies arose from the fact that a small sermon of protest would draw an answer from another wing of the clergy; this in turn would have to be refuted, and the battle was on. There was nothing to prevent clergy other than the two original disputants from getting into the contention, and so we find that the point of the original dispute would sometimes disappear in a cloud of irrelevant dust. One of the most famous private controversies of the reign was the long and violent contention of Dr. Cole and Bishop Jewel. Though this was carried on mostly by means of thick books in which the two men confuted each other point by point, the whole bitter argument was precipitated by a sermon at Paul's Cross which was printed. The equally celebrated controversy between Hooker and Travers was started in much the same way.[27] It was Hooker's sermon entitled *A learned and comfortable Sermon of the certaintie and perpetuitie of faith in the Elect* which drew forth Travers' *Supplication.* This controversy was especially delightful to the lovers of contention because it was so easy to follow. The disputants in this case shared the same pulpit, the one preaching in the morning and the other in the afternoon, and thus the arguing progressed logically, clearly, and swiftly, there being two bouts each Sunday. But since private quarrels did not involve either the state or the Church as a whole, little was done about quelling them.

Moreover not only were these private controversies not prevented by authority, but they were much encouraged by the popular interest in them. People flocked to hear men who did more exciting things than point out the way to heaven, and they read

27. The Whitgift - Cartwright controversy was also started by a Paul's Cross sermon. In this case it was the sermon preached by Bishop Cooper on June 27, 1572.

the works of these same men, thus encouraging presses to print the controversial sermons and the treatises which depended from them. Controversies rarely remained the property of the two original contestants only, but were taken up by others until we find titles such as this: *A Disproofe of D. Abbots Counterproofe against D. Bishops Reproofe of the defence of M. Perkins Reformed Catholic.*[28] If readers could and would follow a theological controversy as intricate as this, it is plain that the age liked controversy, and that it was bound to flourish in spite of any prohibitions and inhibitions there might be.

28. By William Bishop. This treatise was printed in Paris in 1614, but the controversy of which it was a part began in London in the reign of Elizabeth.

# CHAPTER VI

## THE PRINTING OF THE SERMONS

*O Lord, how many excellent bookes are there, which had perished amongst the Mothes and Wormes, and never seene the light of the Sunne.*

THOMAS JACKSON

The printing of sermons constituted a rather large business in Elizabethan England. It has been estimated that more than forty per cent of all publications issued at that time were religious or philosophical in nature and it is evident that sermons account for a large part of those religious publications.[1] The appended bibliography lists about twelve hundred sermons preached in the reign of Elizabeth and printed in that reign or within a few years after it. This number does not include the innumerable translations of the continental divines whom the more Protestant wing of the Church of England so highly favored, nor does it include the reissues and subsequent editions of the English sermons, some of which were reissued annually for a decade or more after the first edition. In trying to account for the printing of so many sermons one might well look into the motives of both the printers and the preachers for an explanation.

Preachers' prefaces to their own sermons are invaluable as sources of information about their motives in publishing, for in these prefaces the authors are careful to give reasons for their

1. Edith L. Klotz, "A Subject Analysis of English Imprints for Every Tenth Year from 1480 to 1640," contained in *Huntington Library Quarterly,* I, 417-9.

lack of that coyness in the matter of publication which was expected of authors ecclesiastical as well as secular. One of the first excuses to be used, and ever the most godly, was the plea of evangelisation. One could publish sermons, protest humility, and stay in character, all at the same time, by ascribing publication to the urge of duty as a clergyman to propagate religion. Consider with what grace John Chardon could send his *Fulfordo et Fulfordæ* forth into the world:

> You had from mee (which you desired) the Sermon preached at Exeter in commemoration of the Citties deliverance, or at the least you received the very summe and substance thereof, which I supposed might have contented you, and the zealous Gentle-woman your wife, without further adoo: but finding you and hir greatly inclined to vulgar profit, and to make common unto many which was then uttered unto fewe, that so the benefit of it might redound also unto many: & knowing you both to bee such as truely, and sincerely love and favour the holy Gospell of Jesus Christ and the Ministers thereof, and seeing your request to stand with so good reason and the Godly purpose, and that my Office and function bindeth mee to doo all the good I can to the Church of God, and that willingly & of a ready mind (to satisfie your honest desire and charitable meaning) have suffred that poore Exercise to bee published which I doe presente unto you as a simple New-yeares-gift.[2]

Frequently the clergyman's patron asked that a sermon be published and saw it through the press, thus preserving the author's coyness and proving his own godliness. James Caldwell thus dedicates a sermon to the Earl of Derby:

> And herewithal it pleased your honor, not only to require a copie of my Sermon, but also give me to understand that you would send it up to London to be Printed, to the ende that the thinges which I had uttered before a fewe at home in your house, might be further published abroade to the use and behoofe of many.[3]

While reticence in the matter of publication was wide-spread among the clergy, or at any rate widely feigned among them, certain clergy there were who dropped all pretence of coyness and sent their sermons to the press without any excuses. John Carpenter was one of these men, and he sent his *Remember Lots Wife* to the press with a preface explaining that writing and publishing was an honorable undertaking and facetiously pointed out

2. Dedication of 1595 edition.
3. *A Sermon Preached before the Earle of Darbie,* 1577, sig. A2 verso.

that he had precedent enough in the fact that God wrote and published the Ten Commandments.

Then, too, a man who was neither the author nor the patron might publish a sermon that fell into his hands to accomplish evangelisation that was beyond his own powers. This was the purpose of John Martin in having Madoxe's maritime sermon printed.

And for that of my selfe I am not so good a labourer in the Lordes Vineyarde, as I wish I were, yea, rather a loiterer, as I wish I were not, . . . I thought it good to sette abroade, in the viewe of the world, to the constant comfort and joy of the Godly, and to the griping greefe and sobbing sorrowe of the wicked, that short, sweete, and comfortable sermon, which that godly, learned, and vertuous young man John Madoxe, in your hearing,[4] preached heere in this chapel of Melcombe . . .[5]

Persons other than the author or patron into whose hands circulating copies had fallen sometimes had a sermon printed with the knowledge, if not the permission, of the author. Such persons also furnished another means of saving face on the part of a publishing author. Even though the dedication of James Bisse's *Two Sermons* may not far depart from the truth, it would still sound very well if there were no truth in it at all.

When I had preached these two sermons (Right worshipfull) divers of my friendes requested a Coppie of them: the which they craved earnestly, & at the last I granted hardly. I had small leasure to pen my Sermons for them, and thought it lesse honestie, and as little curtesie to denie them. But when through importunity they had gotten the upper hande, and recieved my Sermons at my handes, they went presently after a view taken of them, unto the Printer to have them published. They used many reasons to perswade me to yeeld thereunto, but when they coulde by no reason moove me to agree to their attempt, they protested that my Sermons should be printed, though I were never so unwilling, they having the copies in their handes: in the end, when I could nothing prevaile with them, but perforce was constrained to yeeld to the publishing of these my Sermons: I purposed, as duety mooved me, to commend and commit them unto your worships.[6]

More pressing reasons than the pleasing of friends or patrons governed the printing of some of the sermons. Since the Elizabethan sermon audience was not only critical, but even, when

---

4. The mayor, bailiffs, and aldermen of Melcombe Regis to whom this sermon was dedicated.
5. John Madoxe, *A Learned and a Godly Sermon,* 1581, prefatory epistle.
6. Sig. A2 recto.

heated by controversy, hostile, the preacher was forced to defend himself from charges civil and ecclesiastical brought by his detractors. How easy it was to misquote slanderously and maliciously! And since error in the pulpit incurred not only the wrath of God, but also the equally sure and more immediate wrath of Elizabeth, an attacked sermon had to be adequately defended. A sermon that raised a slight quibble needed no further excuse for publication.

> For that this Sermõ may be more advisedlie considered of the Readers, which was not well takẽ part of some of the hearers, where it was spoken: it is therefore thought expedient that the Preacher thereof, should cause it to be put openly in print, and so to refer it, to bee expended by the learned & others of ripe Judgement.[7]

The printers' motive in publishing sermons, though cloaked in many disguises, was simply that of profit. The trade would bear as many sermons as the printers could publish, and the number of sermons they published was apparently limited only by the lack of copy. From this condition arose the many unauthorised editions of which the preachers complained with real or feigned bitterness. The printers did not apologise for these unauthorised editions; ethically the printer was unhampered in his choice of material and in the manner of obtaining it. Prefaces are again the best source of first hand witness of the printers' enterprise. When John Wolfe published H. B.'s *Moriemini* without consulting the author in the matter he thus addressed the reader:

> This Sermon (gentle Reader) having now lein hid and smoothered in a corner these thirteene yeares, or thereabout, since first it was preached at the court, and afterward (upon speciall, or rather general approbation of it in that place) commaunded by some in authoritie, to be then set down in writing by the preacher himselfe: I have by good chaunce, and great favour of a deare friend, now at the length obtained, and thus redeemed for thee from utter perill of extinguishment. And albeit I adventure thus to publish that godlie mans pains, not making him privie thereunto before hand . . . he will in that respect beare the more with me, neither take it indignantly at my hands, that his godly labours are thus preserved for the use of men, then reserved (as before) to be consumed of mothes.[8]

Sometimes the person who without permission gave a sermon

---

7. Anon., *A Sermon Preached before the Queenes Majestie March 2, 1575*, verso of title page.
8. Sig. A3.

to the printer did the explaining. John Field excused himself with the unassailable claim of evangelisation when he dedicated one of John Knox's sermons to the owner of the manuscript which he had borrowed.

> I beseeche you thinke not muche (good mystres Prouze)[9] that having kept your papers so long, and not restored them, I do also now at the length adventure without your knowledge, to make that common to moe and many, which was private to your selfe and some few others. I doe it not (God knoweth) to seeke any commoditie to my selfe; but that I may profite the whole church of God.[10]

Novel titles to catch the eye of buyers were not frowned upon by the clergy. In one case we have the reasoning that prompted the choosing of the title set forth by the author in his dedication. John Stockwood, clergyman and schoolmaster of Tunbridge, published a treatise on August 20, 1589. He realised that August 24 was St. Bartholomew's Day and that the great London fair closely followed. The manner in which he took advantage of the season is nicely told:

> The time falling out so fitlie with the finishing of this worke, and the publishing of the same, I have geven unto it the name of a *Bartholmew Fayring*, the rather by the noveltie of the title to drawe on the multitude of people that nowe out of all places of our county repaire unto the citie, to the better beholding and consideration of the matter cõtained in the treatise.[11]

Printers as well as authors took advantage of the novelty seekers; a few sermons went into several issues, if not editions, to appeal to persons more interested in novelty in the form of a fresh date on the title-page than in the excellence of the content.

> The first question at every Stacioners shoppe is, what new thing? and if it smell of the presse, and have a goodly title (be the matter never so base and unprofitable) it is a booke for the nonce; but be it never so good, if once the Calender be chaunged, that it beare the date of the former yeare, it is never enquired after, it may serve for covers to everie immodest Poeme, girding Satyre, or ridiculous fable.[12]

To attract this type of buyer and to move old stock, new title-

---

9. Widow of Edward Dering, prominent preacher.
10. *A notable and Comfortable exposition,* 1583, preface.
11. *A Bartholmew Fayring,* sig. A3 recto.
12. T. Jackson, *Davids Pastoral Poeme,* 1603, sig. ¶5 verso.

pages were printed and affixed to old editions.[13] This practice accounts for some of the variants in the bibliography.

Except for the actual title, if even that much be excepted, the content of the title-page seems to have been composed by the printer. The texts or quotations that appear on the page are usually not the text of the sermon. If the text of the sermon is there, it is plainly stated that the preaching was upon it; unexplained texts are for the most part decoration, although most of them are appropriate to the theme of the sermon or the occasion of the preaching. For example, upon no matter what text an assize sermon had been preached, we are likely to find upon the title-page some general text from scripture, the classics, or the early church fathers apropos of trials or judgments: "Judge according to right" [*John* 7:24], "Quoties dicitur toties de nobis judicatur" [Cicero *de Oratore*], or "Unless ye repent, ye shall all perish in a like manner" [*Luke* 13:3]. Any sermon on idolatry might have Tertullian's "Idolum tam fieri, quam coli, Deus prohibet", Lactantius' "Non est dubium quin religio nulla sit ubicunque simulacrum est", or "Babes, keep your selves from idols" [*I John* 5:21]. For any sermon against Rome or the bishop thereof, the printer had his choice of those violent passages in chapters 13, 16, 17, 18 and 19 of *Revelation*. For a sermon of very general character, a general fundamental text would be chosen: "I esteem not to know any thing among you save Jesus Christ and him crucified" [*I Cor.* 2:3], "While we have time let us do good" [*Gal.* 6:10], or a more ominous "Babes, it is the last time" [*I John* 2:18].

Another complication in the printing of the sermons was the censorship to prevent the dissemination of doctrines incompatible with the delicate balance of the Church of England between the forces of Geneva and Rome. Direct evidence of this censorship is rare, a fact which is not surprising since the questionable matter was deleted before printing, or if the sermon was entirely rejected by the censor no record of the transaction is likely to have

13. Bartholomew Chamberlaine's *Sermon preached at S. James* is a good example of this; both the 1583 and the 1584 issues were printed from the same set-up of type, and differ only in the date on the title-page.

survived. James Roberts, however, in a printer's *To the Reader,* gives a clue to the sort of thing that was prohibited. When George Estey, a preacher of Bury St. Edmunds, died, he left sermon manuscripts to Roberts in his will together with permission to publish them, which was a windfall for the printer. The fly in the ointment was supplied by the censor.

> Also in this impression, something is kept backe by authoritie, as namely the proofe of the Authors judgement, touching Christes discention into hell.[14]

The harrowing of hell by Christ between the crucifixion and the resurrection was, and for that matter is, a very thorny point and one likely to produce contention. The simple deletion of the matter seemed to the censor a better solution to the question than a heated theological row over the none too clear doctrines of the Church of England.

Sometimes printing was attempted even though the censorship went so far as a flat prohibition of the sermon. Clandestine printing of a sermon for polemic reasons was rarely attempted because of the risk it involved, but there is one good example of a secretly printed sermon. William Burton preached a sermon in 1589 that stirred up hostile discussion. He was a Cartwrightian, to begin with, probably because he had too little wit to contrive an original heresy, and he taught his flock by preaching and by his example in flinging rocks through stained glass windows. At the time of the preaching of the sermon that got him into trouble, it had already become patent that the exceeding hot Protestants were as much a menace to the Established Church as the Romanists and it was deemed high time to quell a few of the more outspoken. How thoroughly Burton was quelled is succinctly told:

> For this sermon the preacher was accounted an enemy to Cæsar, is turned out of living, interdicted of his ministery for a sabboth of yeeres, and by a publique acte, disabled from scholasticall function throughout the whole land.[15]

Such a sermon would, of course, be excellent material for the press if it were not for the rejection of it by the censor. However, in this case, the expected results of printing so far outweighed the risk that printing was undertaken by a secret press, the preacher

14. *Certaine Godly and Learned Expositions,* 1603, sig. A3 recto.
15. *A Sermon Preached at Norwich,* 1589, preface to the reader.

seeking justification and the printer a large sale. The preface served to remind browsers of the sensational character of the sermon and the events attending it.

> As for the Sermon it selfe, hee [the author] protesteth (as in the sight of God) that it is faithfully translated from the pulpit to the pen, saving that some pointes hee hath now more enlarged then hee could then for want of time, but as for those things whereof he was accused, and which were taken so greevously, they be set downe even as they were uttered, so nigh as he could, word for worde, without adding or detracting, without changing or altering, persuading himselfe, that there is nothing to be gotten by licking him selfe whole, as it is thought some would have done: and therefore leaving them to God which would make the worlde beleeve that the hares eares be hornes, calling good evil, and evil good, groping for the light at noone day: he also committeth himselfe and his cause, this Sermon and the event thereof, unto the God of heaven and earth.

Secret printing may have saved the printer, but the author bravely or doggedly held his ground by allowing his name to be used, and the preacher was so well known that the wide circulation provided by publication only invited further criticism and punishment.

On the whole, the printing of sermons in the reign of Elizabeth seems to have been a haphazard business; both the authors and the printers did their work with unnecessary carelessness — the copy was bad, and the printing, if we believe the authors, worse. And an enquiry into the state of the texts reveals them to be rather more unsatisfactory than a superficial examination shows.

# CHAPTER VII

## THE STATE OF THE TEXTS

*Eve never erred, untill she corrupted the text.*

HENRY SMITH

The differences between the sermons as they were preached and the forms in which they were printed constitute a considerable problem. In some few cases we have the word of the preacher that the printed sermon was identical with the spoken; sometimes we have the less dependable word of the printer. But since sermons as a rule were not written out in full before they were preached we are entitled to suspect that the printed text differs in some degree from what was spoken in the pulpit.

The extreme degree of revision between preaching and printing appears in sermons which were transformed into treatises for the purpose of publication. William Worship, in a dedication, reveals an example of this.

> This first Sermon (Right Honorable) was preached long agoe, even in the Minoritie of my Studies. When the yoongnesse of my face, might seeme to detract from the gravenesse of my calling. And through others desire, and mine owne weaknesse, was addrest to the publike view. But for want of due care and fore-sight, it lost the native forme, and came forth disguis'd, in the habit of a Treatise.[1]

At other times, this change of form from sermon to treatise was due not to carelessness, but to premeditation. William Perkins,

---

1. Dedication of Worship's *The Christians Mourning Garment,* 1612 edition. The treatise form of this sermon is now unknown.

the prominent Puritan, was a prolific preacher who had no hesitation in publishing, but he so corrected and radically revised his sermon material before it went to press that neither he nor the printers called the majority of his publications sermons.

These cases of mutilation of form and substance are balanced by sermons which their authors profess to have reproduced fairly accurately from the spoken sermons. When William Fulke sent one of his sermons to the press he prefaced it with this statement:

> Wherefore I addressed my self to put in writing, that which before I had uttered in speaking, observing as neare as I could, not onelye the substance of matter, but also the phrase of words, which I then used, as by reading your Honor can best judge.[2]

Again, Robert Crowley states in the dedication of his one published sermon:

> Yet notwythstanding I caused my Memorie to searche out all her corners, and to bring forth that which she foũd and so have I penned (as my Memorie telleth me) almost the same wordes that I then spake, and in the same order that I then did speake them.[3]

Statements like these are very common, but frequently the author was not quite so sure that the written text reproduced the sermon verbatim. The learned theologian Thomas Bilson, Bishop of Winchester, was more cautious in his claims to accuracy.

> In setting downe the summe of that which I preached, I neither do, nor can promise thee (gentle Reader) the same words which I then spake; I wrote them not; but I assure thee before him that knoweth all things, that I have not swarved nor altered anie materiall point from the methode, propositions, proofes and conclusions, which I then used, nor from the wordes as far as either my notes, or my memory upon the fresh foote coulde direct mee; which I have yet to shew.[4]

In another class are those sermons which have been purposely corrected and embellished for the press, and either augmented or condensed. Of the printed version of his *Parable of the Sower* George Gifford says "I have added somewhat which either thẽ came not to minde, or els time did not serve to handle."[5] Long as these Elizabethan sermons are, this complaint of the restriction of

2. *Sermon at Hampton Court,* 1570, sig. A2 verso.
3. *A Sermon made in the Gylde Halle,* 1574, sig. A3.
4. *The Effect of Certaine Sermons,* 1599, preface.
5. *A Sermon on the Parable of the Sower,* 1582, sig. A2.

time is frequent. Dr. Holland's Πανηγυρὶς *D. Elizabethæ* on the forty-first anniversary of Elizabeth's accession is another example of a sermon which was "augmented in those places wherein, for the shortnes of time, it could not there be delivered". John Bridges, when he came to publish one of his sermons, found that it was very long, but he was not exercised about the matter.

Neverthelesse I was better content to wink at mine owne overshooting my selfe, bicause now it should not be I any more that shoulde speake it unto them, but themselves to them selves that should reade me, shoulde speake it for me, & when they are wearie, lay me aside a gods name, and make foure Sermons (if they please) of one.[6]

As theologians have ever run more to prolixity than to conciseness, it is less frequently found that, in the course of editing, the sermons have been condensed. The title page of George Estey's sermons, however, explains that these sermons have been "more briefly penned by that worthy man of God". More often, an editor other than the author is responsible for omissions; Richard Josua, Jr., in editing George Gifford's *Four Sermons,* even gives his reasons thus baldly: "Marvel not at the shortnesse of it: the cause thereof is this, that the repetition in the beginning of every sermon, to avoid tediousnesse, is omitted."[7]

When a sermon had been preached, there remained more than the preacher's notes from which to reconstruct it if it were decided that the sermon should be published. It was a common practice of members of the congregation to take notes, and a collation of these notes would furnish a fairly accurate copy of the *substance* of a sermon. It has been suggested[8] that in the sixteenth century the practice of taking notes of sermons was an attempt to preserve a corpus of Protestant exegesis. In the seventeenth century the practice became more general, and note-taking was a part of the school training of children.[8] It is rather surprising to see how full and minute the notes of devout Elizabethans who transcribed their sermon notes into their diaries can

6. *A Sermon preached at Paules Crosse,* 1571, sig. A3.
7. To the godly Reader.
8. W. Fraser Mitchell, *English Pulpit Oratory from Andrewes to Tillotson,* pp. 30 ff.

be. One Elizabethan whose diary we have, John Manningham, made very careful notes of the sermons he heard. Sometimes he heard as many as two sermons in one day, and the notes of these sermons fill, on an average, four or five pages of smallish print each. When Dr. King, afterwards Bishop of London, preached at Paul's Cross, Manningham took notes that fill nine printed pages.[9] He begins by analysing the structure of the sermon and then notes concisely every point that Dr. King made. Any person with any imagination could expand these nine pages to twenty, which was the average length of a sermon, and publish Dr. King's sermon; with no notice to the contrary, one would accept it as a true copy.

Elizabethans other than the devout also took sermon notes and recorded them, but they entered only what appealed to them, so that the entries frequently resemble this:

> Colle, Assedeacon of Essexe, prechinge at Powlls Crosse, anno 1565, the xj day of November, lykenyd the pristes unto appes, for, saythe he, they be both balld alyke, but yt the pristes be balld before, the appes behynd.[10]

Here is all that one of the audience would remember of one of the great Paul's Cross sermons!

But most of the note-takers were devout or they would not have bothered, and their notes, if not as full as those of John Manningham, were still valuable as a record of the contents of a sermon. The dedicatory address prefixed to the one published sermon of Symon Presse shows how a collation of these less full notes could result in a printed sermon.

> To his loving parishioners Mr. F. Cooke, R. Johnson, W. Walton R. Knight, J. Gyllyver, & R. Slygh increase of true zeale & endles felicitie. When I understoode your attention in the hearing of this sermon, & diligēce in noting certaine principall points, & paines in conferring togither, penning, acquainting & sending your collections unto many your worshipfull friendes, & at the length unto the right honorable Sir Edmund Anderson knight, Lord chiefe Justice of the common Pleas, with intent (as I gesse) to make my simple skill liked and allowed of them, I thought it my duty to accept your endevour very kindly, and to requite you with procuring the same sermon to be imprinted, that all men might give you deserved commendations, and note your names amongst the number of vigilant hearers to your immortall praise.[11]

---

9. *Diary,* pp. 64 ff.
10. Stow, *Memoranda,* p. 133.
11. *A Sermon Preached at Eggington,* 1596.

This preface, however, is unusual in that the congregation's notes are highly spoken of, for while a great many prefaces to Elizabethan sermons in print tell of notes taken by members of the congregation that were used by the preacher in preparing the sermons for the press, few of them go into any detail about the notes that they mention except to say that they were failures as true transcriptions of the sermons. This preface to Bishop Thomas Cooper's sermon preached August 28, 1575 is characteristic of the passing and derogatory mention made of auditors' notes:

> To the Reader: Whẽ I perceived the ernest good will of some, which tooke paines very busilie to get this sermon so exquisitely penned, as it was pithilie spoke, & had the view of the halfe (& as it were the maimed copie) of the same more zealously then skilfully collected: I (into whose handes by the meanes of a friende this true and perfecte copie came) thought my selfe to be blame worthie, if I should denie to further the honest desire of welmeaning christians. . . .[12]

But by what means the sermons came to be thus "exquisitely penned" we do not know, nor are we told how the "true and perfecte" copy came into being. These are matters for speculation.

Presumably these notes, like those of Manningham and other sermon-connoisseurs, were written in longhand, but it is possible, at least after 1588, when Dr. Timothy Bright published his *Characterie,* the earliest known English system of stenography, (or even before that date if you think it preposterous that shorthand simply sprang out of the blue on a certain given date) that some of them had been made in shorthand. In a few printed sermons the reader is notified that a shorthand writer took down the preacher's words at the time of the delivery of the sermon, either by a statement to that effect on the title-page[13] or by a confessional preface, like that addressed to "the Christian Reader" by Anthony Tyrell in 1589:

12. This unsigned preface is probably by the printer.
13. Cf. full titles of Egerton, *An Ordinary Lecture;* Smith, *The Affinitie of the Faithful* (2nd edition), *A Sermon of the Benefite of Contentation, The Examination of Usury, A Fruitfull Sermon,* and Tyrell, *A Fruitfull Sermon of July 13, 1589.*

> The cause therefore why it [this sermon] is come forth, in brief, was this. At the time I made my exhortation publicklie in Christ his Church in London, my wordes were no soner out of my mouth but a yong youth had penned my Sermon *verbatim* by Characterie, an art newly invented. It was this youthes pleasure, for the manifesting of his skill in that swift kind of writing, to publish my Sermon in print.[14]

Possibly other printed sermons in which no allusion is made to the mode of transferring the preacher's words to paper likewise rest upon shorthand reports, for stenography was peculiarly suitable for this purpose; there is abundant evidence of the practice in the seventeenth century,[15] and even in 1593 it was sufficiently common to move a printer to advertise one of his sermons as *not* having been written up from shorthand notes:

> Taken it was not from the Preachers mouth by any fond or new found Characterisme (which to the great prejudice of some worthie and learned, hath of late verie pitifully blemished some part of their labours this way with intollerable mutilations): but set down at their desire, who might herein command, by the Authors owne pen.[16]

Moreover, some printed sermons contain equivocal statements such as "taken by pen", "penned from his mouth", "taken from the mouth of our preacher", which may refer to either longhand or shorthand transcription. For example, the title-page of George Gifford's *Foure Sermons* (1582) contains the tantalizing statement that these sermons were "penned from his mouth" and is followed by a preface which mentions the mode of transcription again and at greater length, but with equal ambiguity:

> Having therefore of late a kinsman at home with me, who being, somewhat of a readie hande, hath taken from the mouth of our preacher, certaine of the Sermons which hee hath preached, whiche beeing againe overseene and corrected, I thought it my dutie, to offer them unto your honor.

The title-page of Edward Philips' *Certaine godly and learned Sermons* (1605), states that these thirty-one sermons were "taken by pen of H. Yelverton of Grayes Inne Gent." This is presumably Henry (later Sir Henry) Yelverton, a distinguished lawyer

14. *A Fruitfull Sermon,* sig. A6 recto and verso.
15. Cf. W. Fraser Mitchell, *op. cit.*
16. L. S., *Resurgendum,* 1593 or before, sig. A3 recto.

who became attorney-general; whether he was a shorthand writer I cannot say. It is difficult to judge from the printed sermons alone how far shorthand was used in bringing sermons to the press. One can be certain only about those which specifically state that they are derived from shorthand notes, but considerable further possibilities remain.

Curiously enough, the subject of shorthand transcripts of Elizabethan sermons has recently received considerable attention from students of Shakespeare. In order to estimate the likelihood that the bad quartos of Shakespeare's plays could have been constructed from a shorthand-writer's notes, they have investigated the Elizabethan systems of shorthand and a number of transcripts made by them, including a few sermons. Thus there is a considerable literature on Stephen Egerton's one printed sermon,[17] and one of Henry Smith's sermons has even been reprinted.[18] The question proposed by this investigation, whether any Elizabethan system of shorthand was capable of producing an accurate report,

---

17. Cf. H. T. Price, "Another Shorthand Sermon", *Essays and Studies in English and Comparative Literature, by Members of the English Department of the University of Michigan,* X (1927), 161-181. The revised edition of this sermon, published in 1603, fourteen years after the first edition, which is said to have been "now again perused, corrected and amended by the Author", is a very uncertain test indeed of the accuracy of the reporter whose notes were the basis of the first edition. This is an instance of literary and doctrinal revision, not of the substitution of an authentic for an inauthentic text, or of a more authentic for a less authentic. A question mark should be put after Professor Price's statement that the 1589 edition of Egerton's sermon is "the earliest shorthand report that we possess in any modern language" (*op. cit.*, p. 162). This may or may not be true, but it is rendered highly doubtful by the fact that we do not know when this sermon of Egerton's was preached. It may or may not have been preached before Anthony Tyrell's *Fruitfull Sermon* of July 13, 1589, which is undoubtedly a shorthand report. Indeed, as early as 1582 we have those *Foure Sermons* of Gifford's which were "penned from his mouth" to reckon with. In any event, it seems entirely reasonable to accept Mr. W. Matthews' supposition that "Private shorthands were used prior to the appearance of any published system" ("Shorthand and the Bad Shakespeare Quartos", *Modern Language Review,* XXVII (1922), pp. 243-62.), so that the publication of Dr. Timothy Bright's *Characterie* in 1588 need not be taken as the earliest possible date for the appearance of a shorthand transcription of a sermon, or a play either, for that matter.

18. *A fruitfull sermon upon part of the 5. chapter of the first epistle of Saint Paul to the Thessalonians, by Henrie Smith. Which sermon being taken by Characterie, is now republished with the authentic version by H. T. Price.*

is still far from being answered conclusively; indeed, the scholars who have written on this topic are drawn up in two opposed ranks: Professor Max Förster and his pupils, Professor H. T. Price, and Dr. Joseph Q. Adams are of the opinion that a writer using Bright's system of shorthand might have produced a reasonably accurate transcript of a sermon or play, and Mr. W. Matthews and Miss Madeleine Doran are profoundly skeptical of any such assumption.[19] With this controversy I have nothing to do, but I can offer the controversialists a few suggestions.

The accuracy of a shorthand transcript of an Elizabethan sermon is almost certainly incapable of verification at this late date because, apart from the shorthand version, no complete and authentic version of a typical Elizabethan sermon ever existed. At the time of delivery the nearest thing to a complete and authentic version would be a particularly full set of notes drawn up by the preacher, but this would by no means correspond with what he uttered in the pulpit. When the preacher subsequently wrote out the sermon himself, it is not very likely that he would invariably be able to recapture the very words he had spoken; similarly, when he subsequently revised a shorthand transcript of his sermon his alterations cannot be assumed simply to substitute what he really said for the errors of the stenographer. Some of them would surely be second thoughts, stylistic improvements, and even prudent qualifications. While, today, an expert stenographer can produce from his notes a much more accurate version of an extemporaneous address than the speaker himself can produce from his memory, in the age of Elizabeth the expertness of the reporter, the extemporaneousness of the sermon, the fullness of the preacher's notes, and the accuracy of his memory are variable factors impossible to assess accurately. Therefore it is to be feared that the variant versions of Elizabethan sermons — one a stenographic report, the other the preacher's own transcript —

---

19. Cf. Max Förster, "Shakespeare and Shorthand," *Philological Quarterly*, XVI (1937), pp. 1-29; H. T. Price, *op. cit.*; J. Q. Adams, "The Quarto of King Lear and Shorthand," *Modern Philology*, XXXI (1933), pp. 135-163; W. Matthews, "Shorthand and the Bad Shakespeare Quartos", *Modern Language Review*, XXVII (1922), pp. 243-262; Madeleine Doran, "The Quarto of King *Lear* and Bright's Shorthand", *Modern Philology*, XXXIII (1935), pp. 139-157.

are difficult to use in gauging the competence of Elizabethan stenographers.[20]

Although I do not wish to take sides in the shorthand controversy, candor compels me to state that the testimony of the Elizabethan preachers themselves is partly favorable as well as partly unfavorable to the accuracy of the reporters. Such differences of opinion are not surprising, for it is reasonable to suppose that in the days of Bright and Bales, just as in the days of Pitman and Gregg, there were various degrees of proficiency in the "new fangle arte".

Unfavorable criticism of Elizabethan shorthand is wide-spread; as we have seen above, Henry Smith complained of omissions and the printer of the sermon *Resurgendum* said that Charactery blemished many sermons with "intollerable mutilations". Contemporary critics are even more downright in their flat condemnation of it, as can be seen by consulting the literature of the shorthand controversy.

Several title-pages state that the shorthand report was examined or reviewed, i. e. revised, by the preacher,[21] but such statements do not seem to be serious indictments of the reporters, for to give a shorthand report to the printer without reviewing it would be as careless as to sign a dictated letter without rereading it. On the other hand, there is more or less explicit testimony to

---

20. Besides the two versions of Egerton's sermon and those of Henry Smith's *Fruitfull Sermon,* there appear to be three texts of Smith's *Sermon of the benefite of Contentation* (1590). The first is stated to have been "Taken by Characterie"; the second, "Taken by Characterie, and examined after", which seems to mean that either the stenographer or the printer or both revised their work; the third, "Newly examined and corrected by the Author". Smith's preface seems to blame the shortcomings of the earlier versions on the printer rather than on the stenographer, though the reference to "whole lims cut off" may be thought to impugn the work of the latter. It reads thus in the 1591 edition (Sig. A2 recto):

> Hearinge howe fast this Sermon hath uttered & yet how miserablye it hath bin abused in Printing, as it were with whole lims cut off at once, and cleane left out, I have taken a little paines (as my sicknesse gave me leave) both to perfit the matter and to correct the print.

As is explained below, there are also two versions of Smith's *Affinitie of the faithfull* (1591), but only in the second does shorthand play a part.

21. Egerton, *An Ordinary Lecture,* 2nd edition; Smith, *A Sermon of the Benefite of Contentation,* edition of 1591.

the accuracy of reporters. The preface of Tyrell's sermon, quoted before, says that the "yong youth had penned my Sermon *verbatim* by Characterie", and the preacher goes on to state further in the same preface that "He that penned my Sermon as I uttered it in Pulpit, did it most exactly, writing it word for word".[22] Moreover, Henry Smith, who disowned the shorthand version of one of his sermons, evidently found that of another more accurate, or at least more complete, than his own version. Smith's own transcript of *The Affinitie of the Faithfull* was printed in 1591; in the same year the same publishers issued a second edition with the following statement on the title-page: "Nowe the second time Imprinted, corrected, and augmented according to the Coppie by Characterie, as he preached it". Whether or not an expert Elizabethan shorthand-writer could produce a verbatim report of a sermon I have no idea, but I think it quite possible that he could produce as faithful a report as the preacher himself with his notes and his memory.

When a copy of a sermon was written out in full, either by the preacher himself, by collators of auditors' notes, or by shorthand transcription, the delivery of the copy to the printer was by no means the end of the author's travails; there were bound to be misprints, bad readings, and assorted other errors, and it was equally certain that the author would blame the printer for them, and the printer the author just as fervently. The author might ask the reader's pardon for the printer's errors even before the printing began, showing the small faith he had in that craft:

> Wherefore I beseech thee (Christian Reader) in the bowels of Christ, to accept and take in good part my travel: and what errours shall fall out in the printing therof, if the Printer do not observe them for thee, yet I doubt not, but thy owne learned wisedom shall easilie perceive them.[23]

But the printer also had his innings at accusations and excuses in the matter; he might add a preface of his own to make light of the errors and lay the blame for them on the author's handwriting or his neglect in not being present at the setting up of the type. A conscientious author would, of course, see his work

22. Sig. A7.
23. Richard Turnbull, *An Exposition on St. Jude,* edition of 1591, sig. A4 verso.

through the press. Printer Francis Coldocke set up a sermon of Thomas White's without that professor of divinity's assistance and thus remarked upon it:

I crave pardon (Christian Reader) for that the Writer beeing full of other businesse him selfe, whereby he could not followe this, and his hande beeing very harde & small, hath bin the cause of some escapes in the print: Yet let it not discourage thee, but take thy pen and bestow the paynes to correct them, and I hope the profite shall make thee recompence. I have not altogither satisfied the Author niether in disposing many things, yet I have done my best, but the matter beeing not muche amisse, our labour is not lost. Farewell.[24]

Printer Thomas Purfoot presents even more explicit objections to the wretched manuscript of Thomas Jackson, who was wisely afraid to leave the comparative safety of Kent while the plague raged in London. Certainly this printer had sufficient excuse for the errors caused by the absence of the author.

These Sermons beeing committed to my care, to be printed, in the absence of the Author (by meanes of the contagious sicknes in London:) I am to intreate thee (curteous Reader) to bear with such defects or defaults, as have passed the Presse, either through my owne, or the workmens oversight. Wherein, no marvaile if we might be overtaken, considering the closenesse of the Copie, and the same not re-written, but delivered unto us as he did set it downe at the first draught, (over-running his noates) and referring us by signes and markes to [things] displaced: wherein (peradventure) wee have not rightly traced him, or discried his directions in everie place.[25]

But an unauthorized or garbled edition offered an excuse for another edition. William Worship, as we have seen above, published a new edition of his *The Christians Mourning Garment* in 1612 because the earlier edition had been garbled into a treatise, and Dod and Cleaver, who collaborated in so many publications, felt themselves libeled by a bad and unauthorised edition of their sermons on the Ten Commandments and they thus presented their own corrected edition to Sir Anthony Cope in 1604:

Sir, the Lord the searcher of all hearts knoweth, that when these Sermons were first preached, it was never once intended that they should come to the presse. And therefore the whole matter and manner, as might best fit the capacity and necessity of the present auditorie. But since some of the ordinary hearers had published their notes (as themselves could gather them in the time of the Sermon) without our knowledge or consent, and many faults were escaped in

---

24. *A Sermon Preached at Pawles Crosse Dec. 9, 1576,* sig. A4.
25. Thomas Jackson, *Davids Pastoral Poeme,* 1603, sig. S3 recto.

the writing & printing, which by dew care and foresight might have bene prevented: therefore both for our clearing, and the better satisfying of the Christian reader, we were compelled to review and refine the whole treatise. Wherein wee have joyntly laboured (as neere as we could) to set downe every thing, without addition or detraction, as it was first delivered in the publique ministery.[26]

Also, as we have seen, Henry Smith issued an authorized edition of his *Sermon of the Benefite of Contentation* only after two garbled editions drove him to it.

Between poor copy, editing printers, bad press work, and the critical attitude of Elizabethan sermon readers, the discouragements to the authors were great. The gloomy, high-church Edward Bulkeley, for instance, was almost reduced to silence by the difficulties in getting a text before the public.

And surely I suppose, there was never age more fertile then this, in bringing forth malicious momouses that are more ready to carpe & reprehend the well doings of others, then any wayes to doe good themselves. Therefore for that I have bene unwilling to be bitten with such Theons teeth . . . I have never published any thing in print, but one other sermon preached about 14. or 15. yeares past at Paules crosse, . . . But that simple & short sermon was so handled in printing, above 60. foule faultes being committed in it (such is the great and intollerable negligence of some printers, which deserveth sharpe punishment) that I have bene ever since more moved to continue Platoes safe course of not writing, but learning.[27]

26. Dod and Cleaver, *A Plain and Familiar Exposition of the Ten Commandements,* sig. A2 recto. The earlier edition of which the authors complain is now unknown. A preface much like this, charging pirates with a very bad edition, is contained in Playfere's *Pathway to Perfection,* edition of 1596, sig. A2.

27. *A Sermon Preached at Bletsoe,* 1586, sig. A2 verso.

## CHAPTER VIII

### THE LITERARY VALUE OF THE SERMONS

*See what it is (good Reader) for a man to loose himselfe in the wildernesse of his owne wit.*

THOMAS BILSON

The literary value of the Elizabethan sermons is most erratic; some few sermons will be found to be truly great and some few others to be really wretched stuff considered as literature, theological values being beyond the scope of this discussion. Between these two extremes lies a great mass of sermons, about twelve hundred in number, of which a definitive review is plainly out of the question. Some of the most common literary traits found in them may be picked out, however, and a general view of this unwieldy mass of individual sermons may thereby be gained.

It is difficult to detect any common or prevailing tendency or tendencies in the organization of Elizabethan sermons. Except for the scheme of introduction, development, and summary (or introduction, proposition, argument, confutation, and conclusion), enjoined by practically every manual of rhetoric that has ever been written, the pattern of the sermons is rarely susceptible of definition. The most common mode of development is that of consecutive statement. In the Elizabethan sermon the art of composition, the art of arranging ideas in a structure of ordered beauty, was practised only in the most elementary way. It was reserved for later times to fashion sermons which, in their disposition of the parts according to a carefully conceived and cumulatively effective scheme, are fit to compare with the classical oration. The Elizabethan sermon is polemical, and the atmosphere of acrid disputation is hostile to the poise and the assurance which seem indispensable to pulpit oratory of enduring literary excellence.

Nor is it possible to trace any noteworthy correspondences between the organization of the sermon and the precepts of the rhetorical manuals available during the reign of Elizabeth. Leonard Cox's *Arte or craft of rhetoryke,* published about 1524, an elementary summary of Melanchthon, and Sherry's *Treatise of the Figures of Grammer and Rhetorike,* 1555, do not illuminate the practice of sixteenth-century preachers in planning their sermons. The contemporary treatises on the art of preaching are no more helpful. Two of these were current in the age of Elizabeth. The first, Niel Hemmingsen's *The Preacher, or method of preaching,* was translated into English by John Horsfall and published in 1574. The second, Andreas Gerardus Hyperius' *Practis of preaching,* Englished by John Ludham, appeared in 1577. Neither of these treatises has any great originality, both being traditional rehashings of Cicero, Quintilian, and other rhetorical masters, who had been highly esteemed for centuries.[1]

The great trouble is that we cannot tell by examining the sermons whether the treatises were used in their construction. Both treatises contain such obvious and self-evident precepts that any one with a modicum of intelligence and tact could achieve an oration or sermon that conformed to their rules without being even slightly acquainted with the treatises. Long traditional practice, university precept, and these manuals all recommend that the preacher compose a sermon that begins at the beginning and ends at the end, by stating a text, presenting divergent views of it, proving his own view, and drawing a moral and applying it to the conduct of life. Hundreds of sermons conform to this type of structure, but who shall say that they do so because of several dull and unoriginal treatises? Thomas Nashe comes nearer to the probable truth when he asserts that men come by their pulpit style by practice and by hearing other sermons.[2] Good sermons

1. For an analysis of these manuals see Marsee Fred Evans' *A Study in the Development of a Theory of Homiletics in England from 1534 to 1692.* This, being a University of Iowa dissertation, is unpublished.

2. *Pierce Penilesse,* McKerrow edition, I, 192.

were preached that conform to no rules at all; Hooker and other fine preachers produced sermons that expound a text section by section and not as one unit, while Andrewes' exegesis proceeds by single words of his text. If the treatises on construction had any influence, it was probably baneful, for the greatest preachers are those who are found to be quite irregular in the construction of their sermons.

Perhaps the frequent informality and the invariable unoriginality of the sermon pattern is not to be wondered at in an age which tended to think of rhetoric as a matter of schemes and tropes, of figurative and verbal ornamentation. In the use of stylistic ornamentation, the Elizabethan sermon follows the course of development of the secular prose of the period. Used sparingly or not at all by most preachers at the beginning of the reign, with the passing of time stylistic ornament attained greater and greater popularity as a result of the same interest in cultivated prose style and the same ingenuous desire to tickle the auditor's attention as produced the Euphuistic and the Arcadian varieties of secular prose. Whether it was legitimate to allure the auditor to listen to good doctrine by use of the more or less meretricious art of rhetoric was a question upon which opinion was divided, but in practice only the severest preachers altogether disdained the use of artifice to interest and impress their congregations. One would not expect the Elizabethan delight in wit to fail to manifest itself either in the composition or in the criticism of sermons, and, indeed, either in the form of decoration of the substance of the sermon with schemes of words and figurative illustrations or in that of the subtle analysis of the text and the embroidering of the explication thereof with learned allusions and quotations which is the hallmark of the most brilliant school of preachers of the next reign, wit is characteristic of the great mass of Elizabethan sermons. On this basis, three Elizabethan styles of preaching can readily be distinguished — in the order of their evolution, the plain, the florid, and the witty.

The plain style is sober, simple in expression, as direct as possible, and free from ornamentation of either fantastic ideas or verbiage. Though it appears, on the whole, to be the spontaneous creation of the spirit of the Reformation, it has closer affinities with the pungent style of Latimer than with the rhetorical style of Fisher, which, indeed, foreshadows the florid style of the Elizabethan preachers. The plain style generally prevailed at the beginning of the reign, partly because of the predominance of Calvinistic preachers and preaching, partly because the awakening of a consciousness of the allurements of rhetoric was a gradual process, but even after the more ornate styles had become popular there were men who continued to use the plain style as a matter of choice. These later plain sermons are usually found to have been written by the Protestant wing of the clergy who stood for simplicity in all things, and we have proof enough that these sermons are purposely unornamented. Let the preachers speak of it:

> Let the sinner come forth, that hath beene converted by hearing stories or fables of poets, I am sure there is none: for faith is onely by the worde of God: or let the preacher come forth that useth such things, and doth it not either to please men, or to boast of his learning.[3]
>
> For there are some which thinke Christe too base to bee preached simply in him self, and therefore mingle with him too much the wisedome of mans eloquence, and thinke that Christe commeth nakedly, unlesse cloathed with vaine ostentation of wordes. Others esteeme him too homely, simple and unlearned, unlesse he bee beautified and blazed over with store of Greeke or Laten sentences in the pulpits: some recken of him as solitarie, or as a private person without honor and pompe, unlesse he bee brought foorth of them very solemnly, accompaned and countenaunced, with the auncient Garde of the fathers and Doctors of the Churche to speake for him: or els he must be glosed out and painted with the frooth of Philosophi, Poetry or such like.[4]

At times, even members of the strongly anti-Puritan wing of the clergy wrote in an unornamented style either for the same reasons as the Puritan faction or for reasons of their own. John Bridges, who was prominent on the prelates' side of the Marprelate controversy, shows in a preface the premeditation of his fairly plain sermon style:

> As for eloquence, here is none: neither I have it, nor my matter desires it. Which though it be not set foorth in *sublimibus humanæ sapientiæ verbis,* yet have it truthe joyned with simplicitie, it is enough.[5]

---

3. Edward Dering, *XXVII Lectures or Readings,* No. 20.
4. Bartimaeus Andrewes, *Certaine verie worthie, godly, and profitable Sermons,* edition of 1583, p. 26.
5. *A Sermon preached at Paules Crosse,* 1571, sig. A3.

It is possible, in this case, that a very plain style was adopted for the express purpose of giving the Puritans, who were sure to answer this provocative sermon, just one less thing to carp about.

But even though a high churchman might use the plain style for one reason or another, it remains a fact that it must be chiefly associated with the more melancholy brands of Protestants, for this was the style of the Marian exiles and of other prominent Protestants such as William Perkins, John Knox, Thomas Cartwright, Eusebius Pagit, Edward Dering, John Keltridge, John Knewstub, and Stephen Egerton.

William Perkins is a good example of this group of writers of the plain style to inspect more closely. He was a very popular preacher with the more Protestant congregations and a leader of the presbyterian movement (out of which grew the Congregational Church, not the Presbyterian Church as we know it). Perkins' sermons are not so plentiful in the bibliography as are those of some other men, for the reason that while he was a prolific preacher and writer of sermons, most of his sermons lost their sermon form when he revised, corrected, and enlarged them for the press.

Although the plain style was no longer in vogue when Perkins was preaching, his style is extremely austere. Perkins was not ignorant of the rules of rhetoric, but he used them only when they gained him clarity and power and never for ornament. He not only was aware of the austerity of his style, but championed it as a virtue just as he championed simplicity in worship. His sermons seem to us to be very zealous, very long, and not very entertaining reading, which is just about what he would wish us to think of them. His aim was to present his particular brand of theology clearly and definitively, and this he has done point by point, drawing attention to the sections of the sermons by proceding from "firstly" and "secondly" to "twentiethly" and upwards. His use of the question-and-answer machinery makes sections of his sermons resemble Socratic dialogues, but rhetorical devices to tickle the ears of his auditors he spurns. The popularity of such a man must have depended upon audiences of ultra-Protestant leanings who were as zealous, and as desirous of simplicity, as was Perkins himself. With such an audience, a man who was learned and grave and evidently fired by a burning zeal needed no pulpit tricks nor any fashionable literary style.

The florid style, like almost every other form of cultivated prose of the early Renaissance, is basically Ciceronian. When the admiration and imitation of Cicero, universally regarded as the supreme master of persuasion and the most cunning literary artificer in prose, was carried over from Latin to the vernacular languages, it became apparent that English was intrinsically not adaptable to the requirements of the rolling Ciceronian period and thus the leading feature of the Ciceronian style left its mark on English prose only in a general tendency towards long and involved sentences. It is, incidentally, one of Hooker's distinctions that he alone of sixteenth-century English prose writers succeeded in reproducing much of the dignified and massive effect of the Ciceronian period. With the verbal elegance and figurative richness of the Ciceronian style, however, it was quite different. The schemes and tropes by means of which Cicero, along with most other orators of antiquity and most of the self-conscious prose artists of the middle ages, had enriched his style were quite susceptible of imitation; they could be differentiated and codified as precepts for writers ambitious to attain elegance, as they were in contemporary manuals. As the striving for elegance and obvious effect which is the first stage in the extraordinary evolution of Elizabethan prose style affected secular writers and preachers alike, the florid style asserted itself in the pulpit. This ornate tendency is visible in the great mass of Elizabethan sermons, in virtually all, indeed, except those preached by the strictest Calvinists.

It is difficult to isolate the beginning of the tendency towards ornate pulpit style, for a pre-Elizabethan preacher like Fisher and a devotional writer like More both resort to the kind of ornamentation characteristic of the florid style. To associate the phenomenon, whether as cause or as effect, with Thomas Wilson's *Arte of rhetorique,* first published in 1553 and in its eighth edition by 1585, is natural and possibly illuminating. For Wilson's rhetoric, instead of treating construction and development, is largely a collection of schemes and tropes of precisely the kind that *Euphues,* on the one hand, and the florid pulpit style, on the other, resort to incessantly. It is possible to illustrate most of the tricks of the preachers by reference to Wilson, and to do so is to emphasize both their traditional character, coming as they do from the practice of Isocrates, Cicero, and the mediæval rhetoricians, and their official character, stamped as they are with the approval of the taste of the moment.

Wilson prescribes the use of allegory,[6] and Archbishop Sandys made graceful use of this trope when he came to eulogize Elizabeth:

> Our Deborah hath mightily repressed the rebel Jaben: our Judith hath beheaded Holophernes, the sworn enemy of Christianity: Our Hester hath hanged up that Haman, which sought to bring both us and our children into miserable servitude.[7]

Wilson advises the use of what he calls "A familiar talke, or communication used". "Communication is then used, when we debate with other, and ask questions as though we looked for an aunswer, and so go through with our matter, leaving the judgement thereof to their discretion."[8] The use of rhetorical questions has ever been popular with orators and it is no surprise to see this figure used in Elizabethan sermons thus:

> Is this the institution of Christ? Is this the Lord's supper? Is this the right use of the holy mysteries? Is this it that Paul delivered unto me? Is this it that Paul received of the Lord?[9]

Wilson speaks of "enlarging examples by copy",[10] which is the heaping up of examples characteristic of the more ornate prose. James Bisse thus amplified one of his sentences:

> Although he were a Worme and no man, the outcast of the people, a Pellicane in the wildernesse, an Owle in the desart, a Sparrow without her mate alone uppon an house top, . . .[11]

A little further on in the same sermon the preacher uses a different type of the heaping up of examples, the much more ornate type that we associate with true Euphuism.

---

6. *Arte of Rhetorique,* edition of 1585, p. 176.
7. *Sermons,* sermon No. 4, §12.
8. *Op. cit.,* p. 187.
9. Jewel, *Works,* I, 25.
10. *Op. cit.,* p. 194.
11. *Two Sermons,* edition of 1585, sig. A3 recto.

> What? know you not, that leaven, and a little leaven, doth leaven the whole lumpe? that a breach, and a little breach doth marre the sale of a whole cloath? That a scarre and a little scarre, doth disfigure the whole face? That poyson, and a little poyson, doth poison the whole body? That Coloquintida, and a little Coloquintida, doth infect the whole pot of pottage? That a hole, and a little hole in a vessell, will let out all the liquor? That fire, and a little fire, is able to burn a whole Citie?[12]

John Carpenter combined the heaping up of examples with alliteration and achieved this effect in a sermon:

> It is good for birds of one flight to flye together, chickens of one hen to couch together, sheepe of one fold to flock together, strings of one instrument to sound in harmonie together, members of one bodie to joyne together, and Christians of one calling to love together.[13]

"The feined Fables, such as are attributed unto brute beastes, would not be forgotten at any hande. For not onely they delite the rude and ignorant, but also they helpe much for perswasion."[14] Thomas Playfere particularly took this precept to his use. In his sermon *The Meane in Mourning* we find that the "libard" kills apes by pretending to be dead; when apes come and "in despite skip up upon him", the libard catches three. He also uses a fable of chameleons killing serpents by dropping "a little drop" on a thread onto the serpents' heads. A third beast fable in the same sermon is the familiar phœnix story. In Playfere's *Pathway to Perfection* a more delightful beast fable is used in which we are told that ostriches when in flight flap their wings so that the sharp spurs in the wing joints prick them on the faster.

Wilson makes much of the figure which he calls "contrarietie"[15] and which was so much used in *Euphues* and the *Arcadia*. The fashion of this figure is mirrored in the sermons.

> For even they, these holy men, or rather holow trees, (I woulde they were holye tres, which are alwayes green,) are like the fayre red morning, which bringeth raine at noone: like the calm water, which is moste deepe: like the greene grasse, where the venemous snake lieth, and the filthye curre maketh his urine.[16]

Repetition is a figure that could be used quite easily in sermons.

---

12. *Ibid.*, sig. B1 verso.
13. *Remember Lots Wife,* sig E8 verso.
14. Wilson, *op. cit.*, p. 197.
15. *Ibid.*, p. 199.
16. Bisse, *op. cit.*, sig. B3 recto.

By repetition Wilson means using one word or phrase to begin several sentences,[17] as in this passage:

By this was Paul put apart from the word. This quencheth out the lust of the flesh, the pride of life, and love of the world. This bringeth faith to justifie man before God, and vertues to approve him before men. This harboureth men in the bosome of faithfull Abraham, whome the ruinous habitation of Adam could not preserve. This draweth men from earthly Hierico, to heavenly Jerusalem, and persuadeth Japhet to dwell in the tabernacles of Shem.[18]

Isocrates was the great authority for using balanced sentences, and Wilson also advises a moderate use of this device which he terms "egall members".[19] Richard Turnbull has many sentences in his sermons like this:

These are they which in the Apostle say, let us doe evill that good may come thereof: let us sinne that God may be mercifull: let us commit iniquite, that Gods glorie may bee revealed: yet is their condemnation just.[20]

A man interested in the fashions of literature could combine a balanced sentence with another figure, such as antithesis, and achieve a more striking effect. This example is unusually pleasant:

For after a long cold winter, a little sun shining is fayre weather: after great sorrow, one dayes pleasure is a paradise: after a long bloudy war, a little peace is a merry world: and after long hunger, browne bread is good cheare.[21]

In the more self-conscious styles of the latter part of Elizabeth's reign we frequently encounter words linked together as a chain. This figure Wilson calls "gradation"[22] and it appears as often in the sermons as in the secular literature. Bishop Babington uses it thus:

And if there the Lord hath changed us from carelesse to carefull men and women, to please him in holinesse and righteousnesse all the dayes of our life, then in this sanctification a note of justification, justification of vocation, vocation of election, and so heaven is ours.[23]

"That is called regression," Wilson continues, "when we repeat a worde eftsone that hath bin spoken and rehersed before, whether the same be in the beginning, in the middest or in the

---

17. *Op. cit.*, p. 201.
18. Carpenter, *op. cit.*, sig. B7 recto.
19. *Op. cit.*, p. 204.
20. *Exposition of Jude*, sermon No. 3.
21. Bisse, *op. cit.*, sig. F4 verso.
22. *Op. cit.*, p. 204.
23. *Works*, edition of 1637, p. 195.

latter ende of a sentence."[24] This figure is more impressive in the pulpit than on the printed page and therefore it occurs often in sermons. Bishop Jewel thus used regression to underline the high point of his argument against the benefit of assisting at Mass:

> What make I here? what profit have I of my doings? I hear nothing; I understand nothing; I am taught nothing; I receive nothing: Christ bade me take; I take nothing: Christ bade me eat; I eat nothing: Christ bade me drink; I drink nothing.[25]

Apostrophe, or "outcrying"[26] as Wilson would have it, is effective in small doses, and it is often used in this manner. Illustration of the simple use is unnecessary, but it might be well to show what a ludicrous howling effect is got by the injudicious heaping up of this figure. Bishop Jewel, who seems to have had little taste in such matters, creates this effect:

> O merciful God, who would think there could be so much wilfulness in the heart of man? O Gregory! O Augustine! O Hierome! O Chrysostom! O Leo! O Dionyse! O Anacletus! O Sixtus! O Paul! O Christ![27]

A rhetorical figure popular with preachers was "reasoning a matter with our selves".[28] This consists of posing questions and answering them. Since it is a very obvious figure, it occurs only in the sermons of men who paid a great deal more attention to their style than to their matter. James Bisse was one of those men and he uses the figure in this manner:

> Wilt thou be clad with my garment? cast of thy ragged cloake with blind Bartimeus. Wilt thou have a salve for thy wound? cut off thy rotten flesh. Wilt thou have a medicine for thy diseases? purge thy body. Wilt thou build? Plucke downe thy ruinous walles. Wilt thou sow? Pluck out the weedes of thine heart. Wilt thou put on a clean shirt? Put off the foule.[29]

The use of rhetorical figures such as these is the mark of the florid style. Some preachers rarely used the more showy of them; others, as Wilson foresaw,[30] delighted in the most artificial extravagances and vied with the avowed Euphuists in the fabrication of gaudy schemes and illustrations. Some preachers used

24. *Op. cit.*, p. 205.
25. *Works*, I, 25.
26. *Op. cit.*, p. 205.
27. *Works*, I, 20.
28. *Op. cit.*, p. 207.
29. *Op. cit.*, sig. A8 verso
30. *Op. cit.*, p. 167.

verbal ornament sparingly; others with a copiousness approaching that of Lyly himself. In the history of the vogue of ornate prose style in the age of Elizabeth its conquests in the pulpit have hardly been appreciated.

Among the preachers of the florid style two men stand out from the ranks; one, Richard Hooker, is notable for the excellence of his writings and for his ecclesiastical statesmanship, and the other, Henry Smith is notable for having a greater contemporary fame than any other preacher of the reign.

Richard Hooker (1554-1600) is chiefly known to most people for his *Laws of Ecclesiastical Polity,* which all critics hail as remarkably fine prose. His sermons are no less great, for he was as careful in composing them as he was in writing his famous polemics. When this statesman of the Church of England composed his sermons, he revised them each several times, giving them unstinted time and attention. Hooker did not preach twice a day simply because he could not prepare two sermons that were up to his high standard.

There was every reason to expect Hooker to preach well. Not only was he a well educated man, but he had what so many potentially great preachers lack — an inspiring and intelligent audience, for he was the preacher of the learned congregation of the Temple Church. In point of style his sermons fall definitely into the category of the florid. They are as highly ornamented with rhetorical devices as any, yet the devices seldom strike our eyes or ears, so great is the weight of the matter of the sermons. To dwell at length on the devices he used or to list the great numbers of them is to be unfair to Hooker; such a procedure would make him seem like a verbal acrobat, whereas he is a grave, learned, and very powerful preacher.[31] It is far better to ignore the purple patches and to reproduce an ordinary sentence. Hooker is in the middle of a sermon on pride.

So that if books, both profane and holy, were all lost, as long as the manners of men retain the estate they are in; for him that observeth, how after that men have once conceived an over-weening of themselves, it maketh tham in all their

31. For an analysis of Hooker's rhetorical devices see Fritz Pützer's *Prediger des Englischen Barok,* pp. 36 ff.

affections to swell; how deadly their hatred, how heavy their displeasure, how unappeasable their indignation and wrath is above other men's, in what manner they compose themselves to be as Heteroclites, without the compass of all such rules as the common sort are measured by; how the oaths which religious hearts do tremble at, they affect as principal graces of speech; what felicity they take to see the enormity of their crimes above the reach of laws and punishments; how much it delighteth them when they are able to appal with the cloudiness of their look; how far they exceed the terms wherewith man's nature should be limited; how high they bear their heads over others; how they browbeat all men which do not receive their sentences as oracles, with marvellous applause and approbation; how they look upon no man but with an indirect countenance, nor hear any thing, saving their own praises with patience, nor speak without scornfulness and disdain; how they use their servants as if they were beasts, their inferiors as servants, their equals as inferiors, and as for superiors, acknowledge none; how they admire themselves as venerable, puissant, wise, circumspect, provident, every way great, taking all men beside themselves for ciphers, poor inglorious silly creatures, needless burthens of the earth, offscourings, nothing: in a word, for him which marketh how irregular and exorbitant they are in all things, it can be no hard thing hereby to gather, that pride is nothing but an inordinate elation of the mind, proceeding from a false conceit of men's excellency in things honoured, which accordingly also frameth their deeds and behaviour, unless there be cunning to conceal it; for a foul scar may be covered with a fair cloth, and as proud as Lucifer may be in outward appearance lowly.[32]

Here are contained figures of speech and rhetoric, such as heaping up of examples, repetition, gradation or word-chain, antithesis, periphrasis, alliteration, and balanced members, all in one sentence, yet the flow of the prose is smooth enough to prevent the devices from being obnoxiously apparent. Moreover, in this ornamented sentence our author has said something, and that in logical order; having supposed a condition, he gives examples of it, condemns it, and draws a moral from it. The sentence is very long, to be sure, but this is more the rule than the exception in the sermons of Hooker.

By the sermons of Hooker it is shown that a sermon that was both grave and polished could delight an intelligent Elizabethan audience even though the preacher had a rather unattractive pulpit personality, for, as Fuller says of his delivery, "He may be said to have made good music with his fiddle and stick alone,

32. *Works,* III, 605.

without any rosin, having neither pronunciation nor gesture to grace his matter."[33] Izaak Walton, in his *Life of Hooker,* tells of this quiet and unimpressive delivery:

His use was to preach once every Sunday, and he or his curate to catechise after the second lesson in the evening prayer; his sermons were neither long nor earnest, but uttered with a grave zeal, and an humble voice; his eyes always fixt on one place to prevent his imagination from wandering, insomuch that he seemed to study as he spake; the design of his sermon (as indeed of all his discourses) was to shew reasons for what he spake; and with these reasons, such a kind of rhetorick, as did rather convince and persuade, than frighten men into piety; studying not so much for matter (which he never wanted) as for apt illustrations to inform and teach his unlearned hearers by familiar examples, and then make them better by convincing applications; never labouring by hard words, and then by needless distinctions and subdistinctions, to amuse his hearers, and to get glory to himself; but glory only to God.[34]

The appropriateness of including Henry Smith among the preachers of the florid style is debatable, for while many critics think his style is rather plain, others, such as Pützer, call his style high ornate baroque. Henry Smith's great popularity demands notice, but it also presents a problem. His first sermon was published in 1589, and by 1610 eighty-three or more editions of his sermons had been issued, severally and in collections. Such popularity with the reading public arouses our interest and leads us to expect great things when looking into his works. We look, and are disappointed — not violently disappointed or displeased, but rather left wondering why the Elizabethans made so much of him, for the word that best describes the sermons of Smith is, unfortunately, "dull".

Smith's sermon composition is conventional; he announces his text and then enlarges upon it, beats down all opposition to his view, and ends by applying the moral of his text to the lives of his auditors. As for clarity, he resembles the early Protestants in his use of "firstly", "sixteenthly", and so on, to introduce the sections of his discourse, and he sticks to his text remarkably well. As for ornamentation, there is plenty of that too, but he uses it in a rather peculiar manner, as though he felt that he ought to use it. Other men use rhetorical devices either definitely for the

33. *Worthies,* edition of 1662, p. 264.
34. Hooker, *Works,* I, 79-80.

effect that might be gained from them or in an amused, playful manner; Smith attacks the problem of rhetorical devices stolidly, as one who might say "I shall preach fashionably though I choke in the attempt." At times his figures are apt, and even poetic, as this:

> Adam did not thinke that death had been in an apple, so you would not thinke that death should be in bread: but as a coale hath fire in it, beside the coale it selfe, which fire doth either warme, or burne; so this meate [the eucharistic bread] hath another meate in it, beside that which is seene, which doth either save or destroy.[35]

More often, the figures are pedestrian and inconclusive, as though not much time had been spent in their choice. When figures are allowed to fall where they may, the inevitable result is confusion:

> As the serpents sting is in his taile, so the ende of sinne is bitternesse, lest he should love the vice wherewith he was once defiled, as they which are once drunk, hardly get out of the seller.[36]

Sophomoric quibblings were quite fashionable in Elizabeth's reign, and Smith's sermons are full of them.

> Now we will enter the lists with our adversaries, and see whether these words doe proove that the breade and wine are turned into Christs body. Paul saith, *Jesus tooke bread*: well then, yet it is bread: when he had taken it, then he blessed it; what did he blesse? the bread which he tooke; well then, yet it is breade: when he had blessed it, then he brake it; what did he breake? the bread which he blessed; well then, yet it is bread: when he had broken it, then he gave it; what did he give? the bread which he brake; well then, yet it is bread: when he had given it, they did eate it; what did they eate? the bread which he gave them; well then, yet it is bread: when they did eate it, then he said, *This is my body*; what did he call his body? the bread which they did eate; well then, yet it is bread. If it be bread all this while, when he did take it, and blesse it, and brake it, and gave it, and they did eate it, when is it turned into his body? here they stand like the Sadduces, as mute as fishes.[37]

Smith has another annoying trick — that of explaining his metaphors, prefacing every explanation with the phrase "that is". Here are three in one sentence:

> If Christ be at your mariage, that is, if you marrie in Christ, your water shall be turned into wine, that is, your peace, and your rest, and your joy, and your happinesse shall begin with your mariage: but if you marrie not in Christ, then

---

35. 1604 *Works,* p. 83.
36. *Ibid.,* p. 285.
37. *Ibid.,* pp. 53-4.

your wine shall be turned into water, that is, you shall live worse hereafter than you did before.[38]

These explanations become ludicrous when the matter explained is perfectly obvious in itself:

The Wiseman saith; *Woe to him which is alone,* that is, he which is alone shall have woe.[39]

All of which is not to say that Smith's sermons are ridiculous or stupid; they merely do not seem to warrant the popularity which is indicated by the amazing number of editions which the Elizabethan and Jacobean public absorbed. The fact remains, however, that Henry Smith was one of the most popular preachers of his day and some reason must be found for this popularity. First of all, he was a follower of the fashions and tried to preach in the most popular way. Secondly, he preached a theology that was very comfortable, for while he would be classed with the Puritans in that he had trouble with his conscience in acknowledging Elizabeth the head of the Church, and in accepting the episcopal government of the Church, he preached with a true Church of England attitude. He did not rant in an undignified manner at either Rome or Geneva; he preached the way to heaven and avoided such unpleasantnesses as hell-fire and brimstone, and he was a gentleman as well as a scholar and a theologian. While Smith is as hot against sin and as sincere as any of the other preachers, he has a more worldly attitude in the matter, and betrays no great surprise in finding that sin is not unknown in the world, nor does he berate his audience as though their sins had resulted from sheer willfulness as many of the more thorny Protestants were wont to do. All of Smith's tactics would be appreciated by a fashionable congregation such as that at St. Clement Danes, where he held the post of lecturer.

One more reason for the popularity of Smith's sermons with the reading public, and it is probably a highly important reason, is that a lingering sickness gave him the opportunity to write out his sermons for the press. We have seen that printers eagerly grasped any sermon copy that they could lay their hands on, and

38. *Ibid.*, p. 10.
39. *Ibid.* p. 16.

in this case the combination of eager printers and a popular preacher who was eager "to doe any good by writing" produced a huge number of printed sermons which the market easily absorbed, and which, in turn, increased the demand.

The witty style of preaching, the style of Andrewes and Donne, belongs to the seventeenth century, but it is interesting to notice its emergence late in the sixteenth. The witty style is as artificial as the florid and at some points much like it, for the witty preachers also employ the verbal figures, and sometimes employ them most extravagantly. But the witty style is to be distinguished from the florid by its minute analyses and subtle reasoning, by its abundant use of quotations, not only from scripture, as is characteristic too of many Puritan sermons, but also, and most distinctively, from the fathers and from profane literature, especially classical, and often in the original tongue, and by its addiction to metaphor as well as to the verbal figures. Moreover, the witty style rarely sounds like orotund Ciceronianism; its characteristic sentence structure, made up of short and disjointed members through which the thought progresses as a series of sharp flashes, is affiliated with the Senecan prose style of the seventeenth century rather than the Ciceronianism of the sixteenth.

Aside from Andrewes, the most admired and influential witty preachers of the last years of Elizabeth were Thomas Playfere and John Carpenter. Playfere (1561?-1609), whose earliest printed sermon was published in 1593, became Lady Margaret professor of divinity at Cambridge and in that position must have been influential in broadening the vogue of the witty style. Carpenter (?-1621) led a much quieter life as the rector of Northleigh, near Honiton in Devonshire, and exerted his influence through his printed works. Quotations from their sermons will illustrate the exquisite verbal ingenuity of their kind. While many clergymen used figures in the pursuit of clarity or power, it is patent that Playfere was aiming at humor or sensation when he wrote these pleasant and characteristic sentences:

> Nay our very reason is treason, and our best affection, is no better then an infection.[40]

---

40. *The Meane in Mourning,* edition of 1633, p. 55.

But to live in the Lyons den, when the mouth of the den was shut, and the mouthes of the Lyons open, this indeed was the life of an Angell, & no man.[41]

Carpenter liked to play with puns and alliteration also, in addition to the usual figures thought meet for the pulpit.

From Lots Wife, is learned the lot of the wicked in this world, with a terror unto all backsliders and wicked Apostates.[42]

He could also heap up examples, not very well related, as well as any of the secular authors.

The polluted vessell is with water washed, the raw flesh is seasoned with salt, the dropping vine must bee pruned with a knife: the weake stomackes must have bitter wormewood: the slow Asse a whip, the heavie Oxe the goade, the idle scholler correction, and the fleshly Christian sower affliction.[43]

In addition to all the figures of Euphuistic rhetoric, Carpenter was able to reproduce the riming of ideas as used in Hebrew poetry, but with consistent excess he is a bit super-Hebraic:

For there is nothing remayning, but cursings in the towne and in the field, going out and comming in, in the basket and in the store, in the bodie and in the land, and in whatsoever is taken in hand: a sick bodie and a faint heart, maymed members and a doubtfull minde: in the morning wishing for the evening: in the evening desiring the morning: vengeance from heaven: an hell upon earth.[44]

One very great preacher may be placed beside these two triflers, but not without a word of warning that he belongs to a world apart spiritually. Bishop Lancelot Andrewes is remembered as a brilliant ornament of the court of James I, but he had been preaching for at least ten years when Queen Elizabeth died and cannot, therefore, be omitted from the bead-roll of Elizabethan preachers. As one of the earliest and the most eminent practitioners of the witty style, he demands special notice.

Bishop Andrewes, like Hooker, was a learned man and fortunately also had a learned audience to preach to, but he had a great advantage over Hooker in that he possessed a most engaging pulpit manner and a fluency of speech which all clergymen might envy. His style is more ornate than that of any other Elizabethan

---

41. *Ibid.*, p. 45.
42. *Op. cit.*, sig. E1 verso.
43. *Ibid.*, sig. C8 recto.
44. *Ibid.*, sig. B8 recto.

preacher and, furthermore, the rhetorical devices that he employs are immediately apparent to the reader or hearer. The metaphysical conceit, high point of the witty style, was first developed by Andrewes, but not until the reign of James; by the time of the death of Elizabeth, however, all of the other characteristics of his very individual style had emerged. His method of preaching was that of verbal exegesis, and no man has bettered him in wringing every word of his text dry of all its meaning. Word by word he attacks his text and tracks down each word no matter where it leads him, which is rather far afield in many instances. This habit makes Andrewes a bit difficult to follow at times, but it cannot be said that he wanders away from his text aimlessly. Latin, Greek and Hebrew were so familiar that phrases of these languages are liberally sprinkled over his pages; quotations stud the sermons like cloves on a ham — quotations from the Bible, the church fathers, and from secular classics ancient and modern. His sentences are as short as Hooker's are long, and have a curt rhythm so marked as to seem very self-conscious. A short passage (not a purple patch) will illustrate both his method and his style. Andrewes is examining half of a line from the Psalms, "Cum occideret eos, quærebant Eum" (Psalm 78:34):

And not only missorted, but misplaced. For *cum occideret,* "His killing" standeth before "our seeking;" whereas our seeking should be first, and His killing come after. This was never God's *fiant,* they must have a *ne fiant.*

Of these two then. First by way of report jointly that *de facto* thus it is—thus they, and thus we seek.

Then if we take them in sunder, and as Jeremy saith "separate the precious from the vile," *quaerebant Eum* the flower of our actions, from *cum occideret,* the dross, dregs, and very refuse of our time. Consider them apart, and shew, 1. That this time is not the time; 2. and that this seeking thus sorted and thus placed is no seeking, nor ever shall find. Therefore, with Asaph's instruction, to settle our seeking upon some other time, and to resolve to begin it before.

Two powers there are in *cum;* 1. a privative, of all times before; 2. a positive of that instant time then. No time before we seek, at that instant time then we do. On which two consisteth *theatrum vitae,* 'the very theatre of our life.' Our case before that time is lively expressed in the words immediately precedent; "They spend their days in vanity, and their years in turmoil in the world." Our case then at that time in these words, *cum occideret eos.* Yea, by implication they are both in this verse; by what they do now is implied what they did before. 1. Now "they sought Him," so that before they lost Him. 2. Again, then "they turned to;" so that before they turned away, and not once looked toward Him. 3. Now "they rose up early," so that before they put it off till twilight. 4. Now "they remembered," so that before they forgot Him clean—no speech, no question, nay no thought about Him.[45]

At other times, when Andrewes was not being so minute in his discussion of a text, his style becomes less choppy although it still is readily identifiable as that of Andrewes. In the following passage from a Whitsunday sermon he uses the conceit of blood crying to heaven. He is speaking of the necessity of invocations to God.

And of all invocations, that which King David doth commend most, and betake himself to, as the most effectual and surest of all; and that is, *Accipiam calicem salutaris, et nomen Domini invocabo;* to call on His name, with the cup of salvation taken in our hands. . . . Why, what virtue is there in taking it, to help invocation? A double. For whether we respect our sins, they have a voice, a cry, an ascending cry, in Scripture assigned them. They invocate too, they call for somewhat, even for some fearful judgment to be poured down on us; and I doubt our own voices are not strong enough, to be heard above theirs. But blood, that also hath a voice, specially innocent blood, the blood of Abel, that cries loud in God's ears, but nothing so loud as the blood whereof this cup of blessing is the communion; the voice of it will be heard above all, the cry of it will drown any cry else. And as it cries higher, so it differs in this, that it cries in a far other key, for far better things than that of Abel: not for revenge, but for remission of sins; for that, whereof it is itself the price and purchase, for our salvation in that great and terrible day of the Lord, when nothing else will save us, and when it will most import us; when if we had the whole world to give, we would give it for these four syllables, *salvabitur,* shall be saved.[46]

Andrewes' zeal has made him one of the fathers of the Church of England, the first great Anglo-Catholic. His devotion, shown in his sermons and in his *Precæ Privatæ,* is such as we expect to find in true saints only. His mastery of English prose, finally, is that of the literary artist.

But even the very sensational witty preachers Playfere and Carpenter were as highly esteemed by their followers as Bishop Andrewes was by his. In any event, no preacher whether conservative, florid, or witty, was able to please everybody. Queen

---

45. "Ninety-six Sermons by Lancelot Andrewes," *Library of Anglo-Catholic Theology,* I, 307-8. This particular sermon was preached before Queen Elizabeth on Ash Wednesday, 1598.

46. *Ibid.,* III, 321.

Elizabeth's taste in sermon style governed the sermons preached at court to some extent, but as the Queen grew older, even her taste in sermons changed and she came to prefer the more conservative types. Subtle ones she always disliked, saying, "I see many ever bold with God Almighty, making too many subtle scannings of the blessed will as lawyers do with human testaments. The presumption is so great as I may not suffer it nor tolerate newfangleness."[47] It took clergymen some time to realize what the Queen liked, and Dr. Rudd in 1596 was surprised to be commended on what he thought was a very plain sermon when he had preached much more ornate ones before Elizabeth without commendation. Archbishop Whitgift put him straight on the matter: "I tell you the queen now is grown weary of the vanities of wit and eloquence, wherewith her youth was formerly affected; and plain sermons which come home to her heart, please her the best."[48] Thus the Queen was always ahead of her time in her taste in sermons, preferring florid ones while plain ones were in vogue and coming to dislike the florid ones long before their popular vogue ended.

On the other hand, men like Thomas Nashe preferred the more ornate types of sermons; Nashe thus comments on the plain sermons of the ultra-Protestants:

> I my selfe have beene so censured among some dul-headed Divines who deeme it no more cunning to wryte an exquisite Poem, than to preach pure Calvin, or distill the juice of a Commentary in a quarter sermon. Proove it when you will, you slowe spirited Saturnists, that have nothing but the pilfries of your penne to pollish an exhortation withall: no eloquence but Tautologies to tie the eares of your Auditorye unto you: no invention but heere is to bee noted, I stoale this note out of *Beza* or *Marlorat*: no wit to moove, no passion to urge, but onelye an ordinarie forme of preaching, blowne up by the use of often hearing and speaking; and you shall finde there goes more exquisite paines and puritie of wite to the writing of one such rare Poem as *Rosamond,* than to a hundred of our dunsticall Sermons.[49]

Other persons objected to the verbal exegesis or Mother Hubbard type of sermon, of which Lancelot Andrewes' sermons are the

47. F. C. Chamberlain, *Sayings of Elizabeth,* p. 99.
48. Fuller, *Church History of Britain,* V, 436.
49. *Pierce Penilesse,* McKerrow edition, I, 192.

best example. Bishop Bullinger of Gloucester preached in this manner and was thus taken down for it:

> On a time he preaching at Worcester before he was B[ishop] upon Sir[50] Johns day: as he traversed his matter, and discoursed upon many points, he came at the length unto the very pithe of his whol[e] sermon, contained in the distinction of the name of John, which he then showing all his learning at once, full learnedly handled after this manner. John, John, the grace of God, the grace of God, the grace of God: gracious John, not graceles John, but gracious John. John, holy John, holy John, not John ful of holes, but holy John. If he shewed not himselfe learned in this sermond, then hath he bene a duns all his life.[51]

If we are to arrive at any conclusions about the literary value of the Elizabethan sermons, we must consider that a good sermon need not necessarily be good literature, and also that a clergyman can be popular without composing and delivering sermons which are artistically good. A delivered sermon is colored by the charm or lack of it in the preacher, and as a good actor can arouse emotions in an audience by reciting the alphabet or plain gibberish, so a preacher who has an attractive pulpit manner can please with sermons that are shallow or chaotic.

The number of clergy, also, who would be able to compose a sermon that would be considered first-rate literature was, as has been seen in previous chapters, rather limited, and the tastes of sensation-loving audiences were factors that would not encourage preachers to compose great sermons even if they could. With the clergy at logger-heads with the laity, and the laity in turn brave critics of the clergy, it is no great wonder that so many sermons of this period are of so little worth as literature. A few excellent sermons, a few quite wretched sermons, and hundreds of fair and fashionable sermons: this, then, is the general sum of the literary worth of the pulpit literature of the reign of Elizabeth.

But even though the literary value of these sermons is admittedly slight, it cannot be inferred that their importance is also slight, for they illustrate a most critical period in the history

---

50. The making of errors in titles and names of saints was a popular diversion among the hotter Protestants.

51. *An Epistle to the Terrible Priests* . . . (Marprelate tract), Arber edition, p. 42.

of the Church. Although church history has been consistently subordinated to the discussion of the sermons, except where it explains the sermons or shows a motivation for them, a dissertation on the pulpits of Elizabeth's reign would be incomplete without some summary of the momentous changes that occurred in the Church of England in that same period. Between the period of the martyrs and the exiles and the period of Bishop Andrewes, the Church accomplished one half of the possible cycle of churchmanship, from low to high, for at the beginning of the reign the exponents of the most hard-bitten and melancholy Calvinism were in the ascendant, while at the end of the reign we have Andrewes and his practical Catholicism. Richard Hooker marks the turning point in this development, since it was in the period in which he was dominant that Geneva supplanted Rome as the chief menace to the peace of the Church of England. He was the statesman who helped make permanent the middle course desired by the far-seeing Elizabeth. Not only did he clear away many of the more fanatical ideas of the continental Protestants, but he saw the value of the Apostolic Succession and of the position of the priesthood as more than a human ordinance. He it was who led the procession back to the Primitive Church. Bishop Andrewes, as Mr. T. S. Eliot has pointed out, marks the attainment by the Established Church of a tenable position. Even the most respected of the English martyrs spoke as individual protesters, but by the end of Elizabeth's reign Bishop Andrewes was able to speak authoritatively as the voice of the Church.

In this same period, the style of the sermon also completed one half of its possible cycle, from severe plainness to the highest state of ornamentation. Soon the cycle was on its way to completion, for the sermons of Donne are the beginnings of the decline of the ornamented styles through Archbishop Laud and Jeremy Taylor to the once more severely plain sermon style of Archbishop Tillotson.

Whether the literary style of the Elizabethan sermons is excellent or otherwise, many of them will be found very entertaining reading by persons not much interested in theology, for quite a few of them contain no more of that divine science than the thimbleful in the text. The historian will find these sermons a mine of information and commentary, while the general student of things Elizabethan will find these much neglected pages of prose a most accurate mirror of nearly every facet of the thought of the period.

# WORKS REFERRED TO

(This list does not include original editions of sermons, which will be found in the main bibliography.)

Adams, J. Q. "The Quarto of King Lear and Shorthand", *Modern Philology,* XXXI (1933), 135-163.

Birch, Thomas. *Memoirs of the Reign of Queen Elizabeth.* London, 1774. 2v.

Burrage, Champlin. *The Early English Dissenters.* Cambridge, 1912. 2v.

*Calendar of State Papers, Domestic Series, of the Reigns of Edward VI, Mary, Elizabeth, 1547-1580.* London, 1856.

*Calendar of State Papers, Domestic Series, of the Reign of Elizabeth.* London, 1856-72. 7v.

Camden, William. *A History of . . . Princess Elizabeth, Late Queen of England.* London, 1688.

Cartwright, Thomas. *An Answer to the Admonition.* Reprinted in Parker Society edition of Whitgift, v.1-3. London, 1851-3.

Carwithen, J. B. S. *The History of the Church of England.* Oxford, 1849. 2v.

Cawley, William. *The Laws Concerning Jesuits.* London, 1680.

Chamberlain, John. *The Letters of John Chamberlain.* Edited by N. E. McClure. Philadelphia, 1939. 2v.

Chamberlin, F. C. *Sayings of Queen Elizabeth.* London, 1923.

Child, Gilbert W. *Church and State under the Tudors.* London, 1890.

Clarke, William. *The Anglican Reformation.* New York, 1900.

*Dictionary of National Biography.*

Doran, Madeleine. "The Quarto of *King Lear* and Bright's Shorthand", *Modern Philology,* XXXIII (1935), 139-157.

Eliot, T. S. *For Lancelot Andrewes.* London, 1928.

Evans, Marsee Fred. *A Study in the Development of a Theory of Homiletics in England from 1534 to 1692.* University of Iowa dissertation, unpublished, 1933.

Förster, Max. "Shakespeare and Shorthand", *Philological Quarterly,* XVI (1937), 1-29.

Foxe, John. *Actes and monuments of matters . . .* (Book of Martyrs). London, 1610.

Frere, W. H. *The History of the English Church.* London, 1904.

Fuller, Thomas. *Church History of Britain.* Edited by J. S. Brewer. Oxford, 1845. 5v.

——— *History of the Worthies of England.* London, 1840.

Gee, Henry. *The Elizabethan Clergy and the Settlement of Religion.* Oxford, 1898.

——— *The Reformation Period.* London, 1909.

Green, John R. *A History of the English People.* London, 1877-82. 4v.

Grindal, Edmund, *Abp. The Remains of Edmund Grindal.* Parker Society, Cambridge, 1843.

Hardwicke, Philip Yorke, 2nd Earl of. *Miscellaneous State Papers.* London, 1778. 2v.

Harrison, G. B. *An Elizabethan Journal.* London, 1928.

Haweis, John O. W. *Sketches of the Reformation.* London, 1844.

Hayward, Sir John. *Annals of Queen Elizabeth.* Edited by John Bruce. Camden Society, London, 1840.

Hoby, Margaret. *Diary of Lady Margaret Hoby.* Edited by Dorothy Meads. Boston and New York, 1930.

Hooker, Richard. *Works.* Edited by John Keble. Oxford, 1874.

Hutton, Matthew, *Abp. The Correspondence of Dr. Matthew Hutton.* Surtees Society, London, 1843.

Jewel, John, *Bp. Works.* Parker Society, Cambridge, 1845-50. 4v.

Kempe, J. E. *The Classic Preachers of the English Church.* London, 1877-8. 2v.

Kennedy, W. P. M. *Elizabethan Episcopal Administration.* London, 1924. 3v.

Klein, Arthur Jay. *Intolerance in the Reign of Elizabeth Queen of England.* New York, 1917.

Klotz, Edith L. "A Subject Analysis of English Imprints for Every Tenth Year from 1480 to 1640," *Huntington Library Quarterly,* I, (1938), 417-9.

Lee, Frederick G. *The Church under Queen Elizabeth.* London, 1896.

*Loseley Manuscripts.* Edited by A. J. Kempe. London, 1836.

Machyn, Henry. *Diary.* Edited by J. G. Nichols. Camden Society, London, 1848.

Manningham, John. *The Diary of John Manningham.* Edited by John Bruce. Camden Society, London, 1868.

Marprelate, Martin. *The Epistle.* Edited by Edward Arber. London, 1880.

Matthews, W. "Shorthand and the Bad Shakespeare Quartos", *Modern Language Review,* XXVII (1922), 243-262.

Mitchell, W. Fraser. *English Pulpit Oratory from Andrewes to Tillotson.* London, 1932.

Nashe, Thomas. *Works.* Edited by R. B. McKerrow. London, 1904-10. 5v.

Owst, Gerald R. *Preaching in Medieval England.* Cambridge, 1926.

Pilkington, James, *Bp. Works.* Parker Society, Cambridge, 1842.

Price, H. T. "Another Shorthand Sermon", *Essays and Studies in English and Comparative Literature, by Members of the English Department of the University of Michigan,* X (1927), 161-181.

Pützer, Fritz. *Prediger des Englischen Barock.* Bonn, 1929.

Read, Conyers. *Bibliography of British History, Tudor Period.* Oxford, 1933.

——— *The Tudors*. New York, 1936.

Richardson, Caroline F. *English Preachers and Preaching 1640-1670*. New York, 1928.

Ronan, Miles V. *The Reformation in Ireland under Elizabeth*. London, 1930.

Sandys, Edwin, *Abp. Sermons; to which are added some Miscellaneous Pieces by the Same Author*. Parker Society, Cambridge, 1842.

Smith, Henry. *A Fruitfull Sermon upon part of the 5. Chapter of the first epistle of Saint Paul to the Thessalonians . . . with the authentic version*. Edited by H. T. Price. Halle, 1922.

Soames, Henry. *Elizabethan Religious History*. London, 1839.

Stow, John. *Annales, or a generall chronicle of England*. London, 1631.

——— *Historical Memoranda* (Lambeth MS 306). In *Three Fifteenth Century Chronicles*, edited by James Gairdner. Camden Society, London, 1880.

——— *A Survey of London*. Edited by C. L. Kingsford. Oxford, 1908. 2v.

Strype, John. *Annals of the Reformation*, Oxford, 1824. 3v.

——— *History of the Life and Acts of Edmund Grindal*. London, 1710.

——— *Life and Acts of Matthew Parker*. Oxford, 1821. 3v.

——— *Life and Acts of John Whitgift*. Oxford, 1822. 3v.

*Statutes of the Realm*. London, 1810-22.

Taylor, Henry Osborne. *Thought and Expression in the Sixteenth Century*. New York, 1920. 2v.

White, F. O. *The Lives of the Elizabethan Bishops*. London, 1898.

White, Helen. *English Devotional Literature, 1600-1640*. University of Wisconsin Studies, Madison, 1931.

Whitgift, John. *Defence of the Answer to the Admonition*. Edited by John Ayre. Parker Society, Cambridge, 1851-3. 3v.

Wilson, Thomas. *The Arte of Rhetorique*. Edited by G. H. Mair. Tudor and Stuart Library, Oxford, 1909.

Wood, Anthony. *Athenae Oxonienses*. London, 1813. 6v.

Wright, L. B. *Middle-Class Culture in Elizabethan England*. Chapel Hill, 1935.

Wright, Thomas. *Queen Elizabeth and Her Times, A Series of Original Letters*. London, 1838. 2v.

# APPENDIX

## A NOTE ON THE BIBLIOGRAPHY

This list is based upon the *Short Title Catalogue* and follows its method of arrangement, anonymous sermons being entered under their titles. It includes, I believe, all the Elizabethan sermons listed by the S.T.C. and in addition about a dozen which eluded its compilers. Including as it does 513 separate publications comprising about 1200 sermons, it must, I think, represent a vast majority of all the Elizabethan sermons which attained publication in print.

Reprints are listed only up to the year 1610. A few publications dated later than 1610 represent, therefore, first editions of sermons actually preached seven or more years earlier. Translations of sermons preached neither in England nor in the English tongue are omitted. Latin sermons preached in England, and translations thereof, are included.

Four publications in the S.T.C. which exist only in the brood of error have also been omitted. S.T.C. 1348, Bancroft, *A sermon preached at Paules Crosse,* I. I., 1588, is the same as S.T.C. 1346. S.T.C. 6696, Dering, *A sermon preached at the Tower of London,* Iohn Day, [1570?], seems to be the result of a clerical error; neither the S.T.C. nor the original cards from which it was compiled gives the location of a copy. S.T.C. 11840[a], Gibson, *A fruitful Sermon,* R. Waldegraue, 1584, is the same as S.T.C. 11839, which also quotes *Proverbs* 29:8 on its title-page. S.T.C. 22705, Smith, *A Treatise of the Lords Supper,* R. Field for T. Man, 1596, has no existence, the date being an error for 1591.

Obviously this list has no pretention to bibliographical finish. It should perhaps be explained that, except when marked "not seen", the titles have been transcribed from the title-pages of the printed copies. Except for certain omissions which are regularly made, the title-pages have been transcribed in full. These omissions are as follows: 1) the name of the author and the long lists of his degrees and reputed excellences, which are superfluous in a list arranged by authors; 2) the biblical, classical, and patristic texts adorning the title-page when they prove to have little or no connection with the text on which the sermon was preached and to represent only the whims and fancies of the printer;

3) the address of the bookseller when this information is rendered dispensable by the appearance of his name; 4) the place of publication when it is obvious; and 5) certain other matter ("Anno Domini", ornaments, etc.) which would lend bulk to the list, but no information of value. All omissions are indicated by points of suspension. Undated publications are assigned, within square brackets, to the years to which they are attributed in the S.T.C.; also within square brackets are those dates supplied from colophons.

# BIBLIOGRAPHY

Abbot, George, *Abp.* An exposition vpon the prophet Ionah. Contained in certaine Sermons, preached in S. Maries Church in Oxford. ... Imprinted by Richard Field, and are to be fold by Richard Garbrand. 1600. [30 sermons.]

Abbot, Robert, *Bp.* The exaltation of the kingdome and Prieſthood of Chriſt. In certaine Sermons vpon the 110. Pſalme: Preached in the Cathedrall Church and city of Worcester, in the time of Chriſtmaſſe: ... 1596. ... Impenſis G. Biſhop. 1601. [5 sermons.]

Alley, William, *Bp.* ΠΤΩΧΟΜΥΣΕΙΟΝ. The poore mans Librarie. Rapsodiæ G. A. Biſhop of Exceter vpon the firſt epiſtle of ſaint Peter, red publiquely in the Cathedrall church of ſaint Paule, within the Citye of London. 1560. ... Imprinted at London by Iohn Day. [1565.] [12 sermons.]

........[Anr. ed.] ... Imprinted at London by Iohn Day. [1570.] [Not in S. T. C.; Brit. Mus. 3205. c. 14]

........[Anr. ed.] ... Imprinted at London by Iohn Daye. [1571.]

Anderson, Anthony. A godlie Sermon, Preached on Newe yeeres day laſt, before Sir William Fitzwilliam Knight, late Lord deputie of Irelande, Sir Iames Harrington Knight, their Ladyes and Children, with many others, at Burghley in Rutlande. ... Imprinted at London by Thomas Purfoote for Lucas Hariſon, ... 1576.

........A Sermon of ſure Comfort, preached at the Funerall of Master Robert Keylwey Eſquire, at Exton in Rutland, the 18. of Marche 1580. ... Printed by H. Middleton, ... 1581.

........A sermon preached at Paules Croſſe, the 23. of Aprill, being the Lords day, called Sonday. 1581. ... Printed at Londõ by Ralph Newbery. Anno. 1581.

........A Sermon profitably preached in the Church within her Maieſties honourable Tower, neere the Citie of London. Before the Right Worſhipful Sir Owen Hopton knight, her highnes Lieutenant therof, and ſundrie others of good worſhip and calling, the 25. of September. 1586. ... Printed by Robert Waldgraue, and are to be ſolde at the ſigne of the white Horſe in Cannon lane. [1586.]

........The shield of our Safetie: Set foorth by . . . A. Anderſon, vpon Symeons ſight, in hys Nunc dimittis. Seene and allowed. . . . Imprinted . . . by H. Iackſon. 1581.

Andrewes, Bartimaeus. Certaine verie worthie, godly and profitable Sermons, vpon the fifth Chapiter of the Songs of Solomon: . . . Publiſhed at the earneſt and long requeſt of ſundrie well minded Chriſtians. . . .Printed by Robert Waldegraue, for Thomas man. 1583. [5 sermons.]

........[Anr. ed.] . . . Printed by Iohn Danter: for Thomas Man. 1595.

Andrewes, Lancelot, *Bp.* XCVI. sermons by the right honorable and reverend father in God, Lancelot Andrewes, late Lord Biſhop of Wincheſter. Publiſhed by His Majesties ſpeciall Command. London, Printed by George Miller, for Richard Badger. MDCXXIX. [16 of these are Elizabethan.]

........The wonderfull Combate (for Gods glorie and Mans ſaluation) betweene Christ and Satan. Opened in ſeuen moſt excelent, learned and zealous Sermons, vpon the Temptations of Christ, in the wildernes, &c. Seene and allowed. London Printed by Iohn Charlwood for Richard Smith: . . . 1592.

Arthington, Henry. The exhortation of Salomon. By H. A. London, Printed for Cuthbert Burby. 1594.

B., H. *Moriemini.* A verie profitable sermon preached before her Maieſtie at the Court, about xiii yeares ſince: By H. B. London, Printed by Iohn Wolfe. 1593.

Babington, Gervase, *Bp.* The workes of the right reverend father in God Gervase Babington, late Biſhop of Worcester. . . . Printed by George Eld, for Henry Fetherstone. 1615.

........[Anr. ed.] . . . Printed by George Eld, . . . by the Aſſignement of Thomas Chard. 1615.

........A Funeral Sermon. Preached . . . a little before his tranſlation to Exeter, in the hearing of moſt of the Knights and Gentleman of that Dioceſſe. And at his remooue penned and Printed aſwell for a teſtimony of his true good will vnto them and the whole Country, as alſo to be an induring remembrance, if God pleaſe, for the preſeruation of loue and amity amongst them, and the carefull auoyding of ſuch hindrances of the ſame, as in the Sermon it ſelfe are noted and mentioned. . . . Printed by I. Roberts, for Thomas Charde. 1595.

........A sermon Preached at Paules Croſſe the ſecond Sunday in Mychaelmas tearme laſt. 1590. . . . Not printed before this 23. of Auguſt. 1591. Imprinted at London by Thomas Eſte, dwelling in Alderſgate ſtreete at the ſigne of the black Horſe, and are there to be ſould.

........[Anr. ed.] . . . Imprinted at London by Thomas Eſte, dwelling in Alderſgate ſtreete. 1599.

........A sermon preached at the court at Greenewich the xxiiii of May, 1591. . . . Imprinted at London by Richard Field for Thomas Chard. 1591.

........Bancroft, Richard, *Abp.* A sermon preached at Paules Croſſe the 9. of Februarie, being the first Sunday in the Parleament, Anno. 1588. . . . Wherein ſome things are now added, which then were omitted, either through want of time, or default in memorie. . . . Imprinted at London, by I. I. for Gregorie Seton, . . . 1588.

........[Anr. ed.] . . . Imprinted at London, by E. B. for Gregorie Seton, . . . 1588.

Bankes, Thomas. Celebris ad Clerum Concio. Iamdudum Cantabrigiæ habita, toti Choro Eccleſiaſtico congrua, perinde vt concinnata, huiuſmodi titulo (iuxta-textum) expreſse inſignienda ſagena; dextre ſatis a ſeptemplici ſua fæce, & illuuie abſterſa. . . . Impreſſum per N. Okes. 1611.

........A verie godly, learned, and fruitfull Sermon againſt the bad ſpirits of Malignitie, Malice, and vnmercifulneſſe. Publikely preached by Thomas Bankes, . . . Seene and allowed. London Printed by Iohn Wolfe, . . . 1586.

Barker, Laurence. Christs checke to S. Peter for his curious queſtion, out of thoſe words in Saint Iohn: Quid ad te? Begun in Paules Church on S. Iohns day the Euangelist. 1597. out of part of the Goſpel appointed for that day, and proſecuted the ſame day this yeare 1598. in the ſame place, and elſe where at other times in ſixe ſeueral Sermons. At London Printed by P. S. for Cuthbert Burbie, and Thomas Goſſon. 1599.

........[Anr. ed.] . . . Printed by Thomas Purfoot for Cuthbert Burbie, . . . 1600.

Barlow, William, *Bp. of Lincoln.* The eagle and the body; Described in One Sermon Preached Before Queene Elizabeth of precious memorie, in Lent. Anno. 1601. . . . Printed for Matthew Law, . . . 1609.

........A Sermon preached at Paules Croſſe, on the firſt Sunday in Lent; Martii 1. 1600 With a ſhort diſcourſe of the late Earle of Eſſex his confeſsion, and penitence, before and at the time of his death. By William Barlow Doctor of Diuinitie. Whereunto is annexed a true copie, in ſubſtance, of the behauiour, ſpeache, and a prayer of the ſaid Earle at the time of his execution. . . . Printed for Mathew Law, . . . 1601.

Beatniffe, John. A sermon preached at Torceter, in the Countie of Northampton the 8. of Iune, Anno Dom. 1588. at the viſitation of the right reuerend Father in God, the Biſhop of Peeterborow, . . . Printed by Iohn Chatlewood for Roger Ward. 1590.

Bedel, Henry. A Sermon exhortyng to pitie the poore. Preached the .25. of Nouember Anno .1571. at Chriſts Churche in London, By Henry Bedell Vicar there, which treatiſe maye well be called the mouth of the poore. Imprinted at London by Iohn Audely. [1572.]

........[Anr. ed.] . . . Imprinted at London by Iohn Awdely. [1573.]

Bentham, Thomas, *Bp.* A notable and comfortable expoſition, vpon the fourth of Mathew; concerning the tentations of Christ, Preached in S. Peters Church, in Oxenford; . . . Printed by Robert Walde-graue, . . . [Bef. 1578?]

Bilson, Thomas, *Bp.* The effect of certaine Sermons touching the full redemption of mankind by the death and bloud of Christ Jesus: wherein Besides the merite of Chriſts ſuffering, the manner of his offering, the power of his death, the comfort of his Croſſe, the glorie of his reſurrection, Are handled, What paines Chriſt ſuffered in his ſoule on the Croſſe: Together, With the place and purpoſe of his deſcent to hel after death: Preached at Paules Croſſe and elſe where in London, . . . With a concluſion to the Reader for the cleering of certaine obiections made againſt the ſaid doctrine. . . . Peter Short for Walter Burre, . . . 1599.

Bisse, James. Two sermons preached, the one at Paules Croſſe the eight of Ianuarie 1580. The other, at Chriſtes Churche in London the ſame day in the after-noone: . . . Imprinted at London, by Thomas Woodcocke. 1581.

........[Anr. ed.] . . . Printed by Robert waldegraue, for Thomas Woodcoke, . . . 1585.

Bland, Tobias. A baite for Momus, So called vpon occaſion of a Sermon at Bedford iniuriously traduced by the factious. Now not altered but augmented. With a brief Patrocinie of the lawfull vse of Philoſophie in the more ſerious and ſacred ſtudie of diuinitie. . . . Printed by Iohn Wolfe, 1589.

Bradley, Francis. A godly sermon preached before the right Worſhipfull Edward Cooke Eſquier, Atturney Generall vnto the Queens most excellent Maiestie, and others of Worſhip, in Tittleſhall in Norfolke: . . . Imprinted at London by Felix Kingston, for Thomas Man. 1600.

Brasbridge, Thomas. Abdias the Prophet, Interpreted by T. B. . . . Seene and allowed according to the order appoynted. Imprinted at London by Henry Binneman, for George Biſhop. 1574.

Bridges, John, *Bp.* A Sermon, preached at Paules Croſſe on the Monday in Whitſon weeke Anno Domini .1571. Entreating on this Sentence Sic Deus dilexit mundum, vt daret vnigenitum filium ſuum, vt omnis qui credit in eũ non pereat, ſed habeat vitam æternam. . . . Preached and augmented by Iohn Bridges. . . . Printed by Henry Binneman for Humfrey Toy. [1571.]

Bruce, Robert. Sermons preached in the Kirk of Edinburgh, . . . as they wer received from his mouth: Meet to comfort all ſik as are troubled, ather in bodie or minde. . . . Edinburgh Printed be Robert Walde-graue, Printer to the Kings Majeſtie. 1591. Cum priuilegio Regali. [11 sermons.]

........Sermons vpon the Sacrament of the Lords Supper: preached in the Kirk of Edinburgh be M. Robert Bruce, . . . at the time of the celebration of the Supper, as they were receaued from his mouth At Edinburgh Printed by Robert Walde-graue, Printer to the Kings Maieſtie. Cum Priuilegio Regali. [1591?] [5 sermons.]

........The way to true peace and rest. Deliuered at Edinborough

In XVI Sermons: on the Lords Supper: Hezechiahs Sickneffe: and other felect Scriptures. . . . London. Printed by R. Field for Thomas Man and Ionas Man, . . . 1617.

Bulkley, Edward. A Sermon preached the 30. of Ianuary laft at Bletfoe, before the Lord Sain-Iohn and others, Concerning the doctrine of the Sacrament of Chriftes body and blood, Wherein the truth is confirmed, and the errors thereof confuted, . . . Printed by Iohn Wolfe for George Bifhop. 1586.

Burton, William. A caueat for Suerties. Two Sermons of Suertifhip, made in Briftoll, . . . Printed by Richard Field, for Tobie Cooke . . . 1593.

........Dauids evidenece or the assurance of Gods love. R. Field for T. Cooke, 1592. [Not seen.]

........[Anr. ed.] Dauids Euidence, Or, The affurance of Gods loue: Declared in feauen Sermons vpon the three laft verfes of the 41. Pfalme. . . . Seene and allowed. Printed at London for Iohn Hardie, . . . 1596.

........Dauids Thankfgiuing for the Arraignement of the Man of Earth, fet forth in two Sermons by W. B. The firft Sermon fheweth the manner of Dauids thankfgiuing, and containeth many comfortable points neceffarie for afflicted confciences. The fecond Sermon fetteth forth the matter it felfe, for which Dauid giueth thanks and that is The Arraignement of the Man of Earth, . . . Imprinted at London by Richard Bradocke, for I. B. . . . 1598.

........[Anr. ed.] . . . Wherevnto are newly adioyned two other Sermons of the Tryall of Faith: whereby euery man may learne how to know whether he haue the true iuftifying faith vnto faluation or no. By the faid Author. Imprinted at London for George Potter, . . . 1602.

........The rowsing of the sluggard, in seuen sermons. A. Islip for T. Man, 1595. [Not seen.]

........[Anr. ed.] The rowsing of the sluggard, in 7. Sermons. Publifhed at the request of diuers godlie and well affected. . . . Printed by the Widow Orwin for Thomas Man. 1595.

........A sermon preached In the Cathedrall Church in Norwich, the xxi day of December, 1589. . . . And publifhed for the fatisfying of ſome which took offence thereat [No place, printer, or date.]

........Ten sermons vpon the firſt, ſecond, third and fourth verſes of the ſixt of Mathew. . . . Whereunto is annexed another Treatiſe called the anatomie of Belial: Set foorth in ten Sermons vpon the 12. 13. 14. and 15 verſes of the 6. Chapter of the Prouerbes of Salomon. Imprinted at London by Richard Field for Thomas Man. 1602. [20 sermons.] [Huntington's 4165[a]?]

Bush, Edward. A sermon preached at Pauls Croſſe on trinity ſunday. 1571. By E. B. Imprinted at London by Iohn Awdely. 1576.

Butler, ........ A learned and notable sermon vpon the text vos autem non sic. But you not ſo. Lately preached vpon ſpeciall occaſion, by M. ——— Butler of Owndell, in S. Maries Church in the Vniuerſity of Cambridge: and ſuccinctly debating the chiefe matters, which are now in queſtion in the Church of England. . . . Printed by Iohn Wolfe. 1593.

Caldwell, John. A Sermon preached before the right honorable Earle of Darbie, and diuers others aſſembled in his honors Chappell at Newparke in Lankaſhire, the ſecond of Ianuarie. . . . 1577. . . . Imprinted at London by Thomas Eaſt: the xiiii day of March, 1577.

Carew, Thomas, of Bilston in Suffolk. Certaine godly and neceſſarie Sermons, preached by M. Thomas Carew . . . Printed for George Potter, . . . 1603. [9 sermons.]

........Foure godly and profitable Sermons preached by Mr. Thomas Carew. . . . Imprinted by G. S. For George Potter. . . . 1605.

Carpenter, John. Remember Lots wife. Two godly and fruitfull Sermons verie conuenient for this our time: lately preached on a Sunday in the Cathedral Church of S. Peters in Exceſter: the one, in the forenoone: the other in the afternoone the ſame day. . . . Printed by Thomas Orwin, and are to be ſolde by Edward White . . . 1588.

Carr, R. A Godly learned and fruitfull Sermon. Made vpon the fourteenth of Iohn in which is plainely ſet foorth the true looue of Christ, the markes whereby the Children of God are knowen and the commoditie which that looue bringeth. By

R. C. 1584. . . . Printed for Thomas Lawe, and Thomas Nelson: . . . [1584?] [Not in S. T. Cat.; Lambeth 29. 8. 15. No. 14.]

Cartwright, Thomas. A commentary vpon the epistle of Saint Paule written to the Colossians. Preached By Thomas Cartwright, and now Publiſhed for the further vſe of the Church of God. . . . Printed by Nicholas Okes, and are to be ſold by George Norton, . . . 1612. [31 sermons.]

Chaderton, Laurence. An excellent and godly Sermon, moſt needefull for this time, wherein we liue in all ſecuritie and ſinne, to the great diſhonour of God, and contempt of his holy word. Preached at Paules Croſſe the xxvi daye of October, An. 1578. . . . Imprinted at London by Chriſtopher Barker, Printer to the Queenes Maieſtie. [1578?]

........[Anr. ed.] . . . Chriſtopher Barker, . . . 1580.

........A fruitfull Sermon, vpon the 3. 4. 5. 6. 7. and 8. verſes, of the 12. Chapiter of the Epistle of S. Paul to the Romanes, very neceſſary for theſe times to be read of all men, for their further inſtruction and edification, in things concerning their faith and obedience to ſaluation. . . . Printed by Robert Walde-graue. 1584. [Text not in B L]

........[Anr. ed.] . . . concerning their fayrh [sic] and obedience . . . Printed by Robert Walde-graue. 1584. [Text in B L] [Not in S. T. Cat.; Lambeth 29. 9. 5.]

........[Anr. ed.] . . . Printed by Robert Walde-graue. 1586.

........[Anr. ed.] . . . Printed for Robert Walde-graue. 1589.

Chamberlaine, Bartholomew. A sermon preached at S. Iames, before the right Honorable Lordes of her Maieſties priuie Councel, the 25. of April. 1580. . . . Imprinted by Iohn Wolfe. 1583.

........[Anr. ed.] . . . Imprinted by Iohn Wolfe. 1584.

........A Sermon preached at Farington in Barkeſhire, the ſeuenteene of Februarie, 1587. At the buriall of the right Honorable the Ladie Anne Countes of Warwicke, daughter to the Duke of Sommerſet his grace, and widowe of the right worſhipfull Sir Edward Vmpton knight. . . . Printed by Iohn Wolfe, . . . 1591.

Chardon, John, *Bp.* Fulfordo et Fulfordæ. A sermon Preached at

Exeter in the Cathedrall Church, the ſixth day of Auguſt commonly called Ieſus day 1594. in memoriall of the Cities deliuerance in the daies of King Edward the ſixt. . . . In which alſo ſome fewe thinges are added, then omitted through want of time. . . . Printed by Iohn Danter: and are to be ſold by William Barley, . . . 1595.

........A sermon preached in S. Peters Church in Exceter the 6. day of December laſt: wherin is intreated the ſecond comming of Chriſt vnto iudgement, of the end of the world. . . . Imprinted . . . by Thomas Dawſon. 1580.

........A sermon vpon part of the ninth chapter of the holy gospel of Iesus Christ according to S. Iohn: Preached at S. Maries in Oxford . . . At Oxford, Printed by Ioſeph Barnes, Printer to the famous Vniuerſitie. 1586.

........A Second Sermon vpon the ix Chapter of the holy Gospel of Iesus Christ according to Saint Iohn. Preached at S. Maries in Oxford, the 11 of December. 1586. . . . Imprinted at London by Iohn Windet for Tobie Cooke. 1587. [Original title page wanting in copy seen.]

Chub, William. A fruitfull sermon preached in a right Honorable audience, treating wholy of Affliction, both inward in mind and outward in bodie, with the end and vſe of the ſame, as wel in the good as the bad. The parts of this Sermon doe appeere in the proceſſe. . . . Publiſhed at the inſtance of the hearers. Imprinted at London by Iohn Iackson. 1587.

........Two fruitfull and godly Sermons preached at Dorcheſter in Dorſetshyre, the one touching the building of Gods Temple, the other what the Temple is. . . . Imprinted at London, by Iohn Charle-wood, . . . 1585.

Cole, Thomas. A godly and Learned Sermon made this laſte Lent at Windeſor before the Queenes Maieſtie, on wedneſday the firſt of Marche, 1564. . . . Imprinted . . . by Henry Denham. . . . 1564.

Colfe, Isaac. A sermon preached on the Queenes day. Beeing the 17. of Nouember. 1587. at the towne of Lidd in Kent, . . . Printed by Iohn Wolfe, for Harry Carre, . . . 1588.

Cooper, Thomas, *Bp*. Certaine Sermones wherin is contained the Defenſe of the Goſpell nowe preached againſt ſuch Cauils and falſe accuſations, as are obiected both againſt the Doctrine it ſelfe, and the Preachers and profeſſors thereof, by the friendes and fauourers of the Church of Rome. Preached of late, ... Imprinted at Londõ by Ralphe Newbery ... 1580. [12 sermons.]

........The true and perfect copie of a godly Sermon, preached in the Minster at Lincolne, . . . the .28. of Auguſt anno. 1575. Imprinted at London by Henrie Middleton for Rafe Newberie, . . . [1575?]

Crowley, Robert. A Sermon made in the Chappel at the Gylde Halle in London the XXIX day of September, 1574. before the Lord Maior and the whole state of the Citie, then aſſembled for the chuſing of their Maior that ſhould then ſuccede in the gouernmẽt of the ſame Citie. Concionatore Roberto Croleo. Peruſed and licenced, according to the Queenes Maieſties Iniunction. Imprinted at London by Iohn Awdeley. 1575. [The 7. day of Ianuary.]

Cupper, William. Certaine sermons concerning gods late viſitation in the citie of London and other parts of the land, teaching all men to make vſe thereof that meane to profit by Gods fatherly chaſtiſements. Preached at Alphages Church neare Creplegate 1592. . . . Imprinted at London for Robert Dexter, . . . 1592. [10 sermons.]

Curteys, Richard, *Bp.* The Care of a Chriſtian Conſcience. Ten Sermons on the 25. Pſalme, preached in Tewkeſburie in the Countie of Glouceſter, By Richard Curtis. Imprinted at London by Simon Stafford, . . . 1600.

........A Sermon preached before the Queenes Maieſtie, by the reuerende Father in God the Biſhop of Chicheſter, at Grenewiche, the 14. day of Marche. 1573. Seene and allowed according to the order appoynted. . . . Imprinted at London dy [sic] Henry Binneman, for Francis Coldocke. Anno. 1573.

........[Anr. ed.] . . . Henry Bynneman, for Francis Coldocke. Anno. 1574.

........[Anr. ed.] . . . Henry Bynneman, for Francis Coldocke. Anno. 1579.

........[Anr. ed.] . . . Thomas Dawſon, for Frauncis Coldocke. Anno. 1586.

........A Sermon preached before the Queenes Maiefty at Richmond the .6. of March 1575. . . . Printed by H. Binneman, for H. Toy. [1575.]

........Two sermons Preached . . . the first at Paules Crofse on Sunday beeing the fourth day of March. And the fecond at Weftminfter before ye Queenes maieftie the iij Sunday in Lent laft paft. 1576. Imprinted at London. 1576.

........[Anr. ed.] . . . Printed by T. Man, and W. Brome. Anno. 1584.

Davies, Richard, *Bp.* A funerall sermon preached the XXVI day of Nouember in the yeare of our Lord M.D.LXXVI. in the parishe Church of Caermerthyn, . . . at the buriall of the right honourable Walter Earle of Essex and Ewe, Earle Marshall of Irelande, Viscount Hereforde & Bourgcher, Lord Ferrers of Chartley, Bourgcher & Louein, of the most Noble order of the Garter Knight. Imprinted at London by Henry Denham, . . . 1577.

Deacon, John. A verie godly and moft neceffary Sermon, ful of fingular comfort for fo manie as fee their fundry finnes: and are inwardly afflicted with a confcience and a feeling thereof. Preached at Ridlington in the Countie of Rutland, and penned at the importunate requeft of fome verie godly affected. . . . Printed by Henrie Midleton for Andrewe Maunfel. M.D.LXXX.VI.

Dent, Arthur. A Sermon of repentaunce. A verie godly and profitable Sermon, preached at Lee in Effex, . . . And publifhed at the requeft of fundrie Godly and well difpofed perfons. . . . Imprinted at London for Iohn Harifon, . . . 1583.

........[Anr. ed.] . . . A verie godlie . . . for Iohn Harifon, . . . 1583.

........[Anr. ed.] . . . A verye godlye . . . for Iohn Harifon, 1583. [Not seen.]

........[Anr. ed.] . . . for Iohn Harrifon, 1584.

........[Anr. ed.] . . . Imprinted . . . by I. Windet, for Iohn Harifon, . . . 1585.

........[Anr. ed.] . . . Imprinted . . . by A. Hatfield and N. Newton, for Iohn Harifon, . . . 1586.

........[Anr. ed.] . . . Imprinted . . . by Edmund Bollifant, for Iohn Harifon, . . . 1588.

........[Anr. ed.] . . . Hatfield for Harison, 1589. [Not seen.]

........[Anr. ed.] . . . Jackson for Harison, 1590. [Not seen.]

........[Anr. ed.] . . . for J. Harison, 1606. [Not seen.]

........A verie godly and profitable Sermon. [On Jonah 11:8.] for R. Sergier. 1582. [Not seen.]

Dering, Edward. Maister Derings Workes. 1590. [This "Workes" is composed S. T. Cat. No. 6733 and 6730.]

........M. Derings workes. More at large then euer hath heere-tofore been printed in any one Volume. . . . Printed by I. R. for Paule Linley, and Iohn Flasket, . . . 1597. [29 sermons.] [Part 2 is the 1590 Woodcocke edition of the XXVII Lectures.]

........A Lecture or Expofition vpon a part of the .v. chapter of the Epiftle to the Hebrues. As it was read in Paules the 6. day of December. 1572. . . . 1573. Imprinted at London by Iohn Awdely.

........[Anr. ed.] . . . Imprinted at Lõdon by Iohn Awdely. 1574.

........[Anr. ed.] . . . Imprinted at London by Iohn Charlewood. 1583.

........A Sermon preached at the Tower of London, the eleuenth day of December. 1569. . . . Printed by Iohn Daye, [1570?]

........[Anr. ed.] . . . the xi day of Decẽber . . . Iohn Day , . . [1570?]

........[Anr. ed.] . . . the .11. day of December . . . Perufed and allowed by aucthoritie. Imprinted at London by Iohn Charlewood. 1584.

........[Anr. ed.] . . . Printed by Iohn Charlewoode. Anno. Dom. 1589.

........A Sermõ preached before the Queenes Maieftie, . . . the .25. day of February. Anno. 1569. Imprinted at London by Iohn Awdely. [1569?]

........[Anr. ed.] A Sermon . . . Iohn Awdely. [1570?]

........[Anr. ed.] . . . by H. Denham. [1575?] [Not seen.]

........[Anr. ed.] . . . Imprinted at London by Iohn Charlewood, . . . 1578.

........[Anr. ed.] . . . Imprinted at London by Iohn Charlewood, . . . 1580.

........[Anr. ed.] . . . Imprinted at London by Iohn Charlewood, . . . 1584.

........[Anr. ed.] . . . Imprinted at London by Iohn Charlewood, . . . 1586.

........[Anr. ed.] . . . Iohn Charlewood, 1589. [Not seen.]

........[Anr. ed.] . . . Printed by the Widdow Chalwood, . . . 1593.

........[Anr. ed.] . . . Printed by Iames Roberts, . . . 1596.

........[Anr. ed.] . . . Printed by Iames Roberts, . . . 1600.

........[Anr. ed.] . . . Printed by Iames Roberts, . . . 1603.

........XXVII. lectures, or readings, vpon part of the Epiſtle written to the Hebrues. . . . Imprinted by Lucas Harriſon. Anno. 1576.

........[Anr. ed.] . . . Imprinted by Lucas Hariſon. Anno. 1577.

........[Anr. ed.] . . . Imprinted for Thomas Woodcocke. Anno. 1578.

........[Anr. ed.] . . . Printed for Thoma[s Wo]odcoke. . . . 1583.

........[Anr. ed.] . . . Set forth as they were read in Paules Church in London. . . . Newly Imprinted. [1586?] [Not in S. T. Cat.; Brit. Mus. 4461. a. 4. No. 2.]

........[Anr. ed.] . . . Newlie Imprinted. 1590.

........[Anr. ed.] . . . Printed for Thomas Woodcocke. Anno. 1590.

........Two godly sermons. The firſt preached before the Queenes Maieſtie, the 25. of Februarie. 1569. The other preached in the Tower of London the 11. of December the ſame yeare. . . Peruſed & alowed by authoritie. Newly Imprinted. [1586?]

........[Anr. ed.] . . . Newlie Imprinted. 1590.

Dod, John, and Cleaver, Robert. A plaine and familiar Expoſition of the Ten Commandements, with a methodicall ſhort Cathechiſme, containing briefly all the principall grounds of Chriſtian Religion. . . . Printed by T. C. for Thomas Man, . . . 1604. [10 sermons.]

Dove, John. Of Diuorcement. A sermon preached at Pauls Croſſe the 10. of May. 1601. . . . Printed by T. C. 1601.

........A Sermon preached at Pauls Croſſe the 3. of Nouember 1594. intreating of the ſecond comming of Chriſt, and the diſcloſing of Antichriſt: With a confutation of diuers coniectures concerning the ende of the world, conteyned in a booke called the ſecond comming of Chriſt. . . . Imprinted by Peter Short, for William Iaggard, . . . [1594?]

........A Sermon preached at Paules Croſſe, the ſixt of February.

1596. In which are difcuffed thefe three conclufions. ... [Printer and date cropped off?]

........[Anr. ed.] ... Printed by T. C. for R. Dexter. 1597. [Not in S. T. Cat.; Cambridge Syn. 8. 61. 27. No. 7.]

Downame, George, *Bp.* Abrahams tryall: A Sermon preached at the Spittle, in Eafter weeke. Anno Domini 1602....Printed for Humfrey Lownes. 1602.

........[Anr. ed.] ... Printed by H. L. and are to be foulde by Arthur Iohnfon, ... 1607.

Drant, Thomas. A fruitfull and neceffary Sermon, fpecially concerning Almes geuing, preached the Twifday in Eafter Weeke. The yere of our Lord. 1572. at S. Maries Spittle....Imprinted at London by Iohn Daye,... [1572.]

........Three godly and learned Sermons, very necefsarie to be read and regarded of all men.... Imprinted at London. Anno. Dom. 1584.

........Two Sermons preached, the one at S. Maries Spittle on Tuefday in Eafter weeke .1570. and the other at the Court of Windfor the Sonday after twelfth day being the viij of Ianuary, before in the yeare .1569. ... Imprinted at London by Iohn Daye, ... [1570?]

........[Anr. ed.] [Title page wanting.]

Dyos, John. A Sermon preached at Paules Croffe the 19. of Iuli 1579: fetting forth the excellencye of Gods heauenlye worde: The exceeding mercye of Chrift our Sauiour: The ftate of this world: A profe of the true Church: A detection of the falfe Church; or rather malignant rable: A confutation of fundry hærefies: and other thinges neceffary to the vnfkilfull to be knowen.... Printed by Iohn Daye,... 1579....

Eedes, Richard. Six learned and godly Sermons: Preached Some of them before the Kings Maieftie, fome before Queene Elizabeth... Printed by Adam Iflip, for Edward Bifhop. 1604. [3 Elizabethan.]

Egerton, Stephen. An ordinary lecture. Preached at the Blacke-Friers, by M. Egerton. And taken as it was vttered by Characterie. ... Printed by Iohn Windet for John Dalderne ... 1589.

........[Anr. ed.] A lecture preached by Maifter Egerton, at the

Blackefriers, 1589. taken by Characterie, by a young Practitioner in that Facultie: and now againe perufed, corrected and amended by the Author. Herein the point of Restitution or Satisfaction, is enlarged for the inftruction of fuch as are, or may be perplexed about that point. Printed at London by V. S. for Walter Burre, ... [1603.]

Estey, George. Certaine Godly and learned Expofitions vpon diuers parts of Scripture. as they were preached, and afterwards more briefly penned by that worthy man of God, Maifter George Estey, ... Printed by I. R. for Richard Banckworth, ... 1603. [7 sermons.]

........A most sweete and comfortable exposition upon the tenne commaundments. I. R. for R. B., 1602. [Not seen.]

Fergusson, David. Ane sermon preichit befoir the Regent and Nobilitie, vpon a part of the third Chapter of the Prophet Malachi, in the Kirk at Leith, at the tyme of the Generall Affemblie on Sonday the 13. of Ianuarie. Anno. Do. 1571. ... Imprentit at Sanctandrois be Robert Lekpreuik.... M.D.LXXII.

Fisher, William. A godly Sermon preached at Paules Croffe the 31. day of October 1591.... Seene and allowed. Imprinted at London by Edward Allde, for Edward Aggas. 1592.

........A Sermon preached at Paules Croffe the firfte Sunday after Newyeeres day, being the thirde day of Ianuary 1580. ... Imprinted at London, for Thomas Charde and Edward Aggas. 1580. [Printed by Thomas Dawson.]

Foxe, John. De oliva evangelica. Concio, in baptifmo Iudæi habita Londini, primo menf. April. Cum enarratione capitis vndecimi D. Pauli ad Romanos In qua, de principiis & fundamentis Chriftianæ fidei, de vera & fyncera ecclefia, de Chrifto Meffia, eiufque regni æterna amplitudine, atque infinita gloria, Difputatio cum Iudæis ex Propheticæ fcripturæ certiffimis teftimoniis inftituitur. Per Ioan. Foxium. Londini, Ex officina Chriftophori Barkeri, Regiæ Maieftati Tyopgraphi. 1578.

........A sermon of Chrift crucified, preached at Paules Croffe the Friday before Eafter, commonly called Goodfryday. Written and dedicated to all ſuch as labour and be heauy laden in conſcience, to be read for their ſpirituall comfort.... Seene and allowed.... Imprinted by Iohn Daye,... 1570....

........[Anr. ed.] ... Newly recogniſhed by the Author.... Imprinted by Iohn Daye,... 1570.... [Not in S. T. Cat.; Brit. Mus. 4473. c. 24.]

........[Anr. ed.] ... Imprinted by Ihon Daie:... 1575....

........[Anr. ed.] ... Imprinted by Iohn Day:...1577....

........[Anr. ed.] ... Printed by the Aſſignes of Richard Day. 1585.

........[Anr. ed.] ... Printed for the Company of Stationers. 1609.

........De Christo crucifixo concio. Ioan. Foxi. Londini, apud Iohānem Dayum Typographum. An. Domini 1571. Octob. 1.

........A Sermon preached at the Christening of a certaine Iew, at London by Iohn Foxe. Conteining an expoſition of the XI Chapter of S. Paul. to the Romanes. Translated out of Latine into Engliſh by Iames Bell. Imprinted at London by Chriſtopher Barker,... 1578. Sig: ¶4, A-M8, N2.

........[Anr. issue] ... Chriſtopher Barker,... 1578. [Contains additional material (the Jew's confession).] Sig: ¶8, B8, C4 [a leaf wanting], A-M8, N2. [Not in S. T. Cat.; Brit. Mus. 4034. aa. 10.]

Fulke, William. A comfortable Sermon of Faith, in temptations and afflictions. Preached at S. Botulphes wythout Alderſgate in London, the .xv. of Februarie. 1573....Imprinted at London by Iohn Awdeley,... 1574.

........[Anr. ed.] ... by Iohn Awdely. [1574?]

........[Anr. ed.] ... by John Charlwood, ... 1578.

........[Anr. ed.] ... by Iohn Charlewood,... 1586.

........A godly and learned Sermon, preached before an honourable auditorie the 26. day of Februarie .1580. Imprinted by Henrie Middleton for Thomas Man. [1580?]

........A sermon preached at Hampton Court, on Sonday being the .12. day of Nouember, in the yeare of our Lord. 1570. Wherin is playnly proued Babylon to be Rome, both by Scriptures and Doctors.... Imprynted at London by Iohn Awdely. [1571.]

........[Anr. ed.] ... Imprynted at London by Iohn Awdely. [1572.]

........[Anr. ed.] ... Imprinted at London by Iohn Awdely. 1574.

........[Anr. ed.] ... Imprinted at London by Iohn Charlewod. 1579.

........A sermon preached on Sundaye, being the .17. of March Anno. 1577. at S. Alpheges Church within Creplegate in London, ... Seene and allowed, accordyng to the order appoynted in the Queenes Maiesties Iniunctions. Imprinted at London for Lucas Harryſon. [1577.]

........A Sermon Preached vpon Sunday, beeing the twelfth of March. Anno 1581. within the Tower of London: In the hearing of ſuch obſtinate Papiſts as then were priſoners there: ... Imprinted at London, by Thomas Dawſon, for George Biſhop. 1581.

Gibson, Thomas. A fruitful Sermon, Preached at Occham, in the County of Rutland, the Second of Nouember .1583.... Printed by Robert Walde-graue ... 1584.

........[Anr. ed.] ... by Robert Walde-graue ... [1584.]

Gifford, George. Eight sermons, vpon the firſt foure Chapters, and part of the fift, of Eccleſiaſtes. Preached at Mauldon, ... Printed by Iohn Windet for Toby Cooke, ... 1589.

........Fifteene sermons, vpon the Song of Salomon.... Printed by Felix Kingston, for Thomas Man. 1598.

........[Anr. ed.] ... Printed by Iohn Windet, for Thomas Man. 1600.

........Foure Sermons vpon the ſeuen chiefe vertues or principall effectes of faith, and the doctrine of election: Wherein euerie man may learne, whether he be Gods childe or no. Preached at Maulden in Eſſex by Maſter George Gifford, penned from his mouth, and corrected and giuen to the Counteſſe of Suſſex, for a Newyeeres gift.... Imprinted at London for Tobie Cooke ... 1582. [Printed by Thomas Dawson.]

........[Anr. ed.] ... Printed by Thomas Iudſon, for Tobie Cooke, and Robert Walker. 1598.

........A Godlie, zealous, and profitable Sermon vpon the ſecond Chapter of Saint Iames. Preached at London, by Maſter George Gifford, and publiſhed at the requeſt of ſundry godly and well diſpoſed perſons. Imprinted at London for Tobie Cooke, ... 1582. [Printed by Thomas East.]

........[Anr. ed.] ... Imprinted at London for Tobie Cooke, ... 1582. [Printed by John Wolfe; not in S. T. Cat.]

........[Anr. ed.] ... Imprinted at London, for Tobie Cooke,... 1583. [Printed by Roger Warde.]

........A Sermon on the Parable of the Sower. ... for Tobie Cooke, 1582.

........[Anr. ed.] A Sermon on the Parable of the Sower, taken out of the 13 of Matthew. Preached at London by M. G. Gifford, and publifhed at the requeft of fundry godly and well difpofed perfons. ... Printed by Iohn Wolfe for Toby Cooke. 1584.

........[Anr. ed.] ... Printed by Robert Walde-graue, for Tobie Cooke, ... [No date.]

........Sermons vpon the whole booke of the Reuelation. Set forth by George Gyffard,...Printed for Thomas Man, and Toby Cooke. 1596. [50 sermons.]

........[Anr. ed.] ... Printed by Richard Field and Felix Kingfton. 1599.

........Two sermons vpon 1. Peter 5. verf. 8. and 9. Wherein is fhewed that the diuell is to be refisted only by a ftedfast faith, how foeuer he commeth either againft foule or body: and that whofoeuer hath once attained the true and liuely faith, it can neuer be vtterly loft, but he is fure to get the victorie ... Printed by Felix Kingfton, for Thomas Man. 1597.

Godwin, Francis, *Bp.* Concio habita in domo Capitulari Ecclefiæ cathed. S. Petri Exon. Aug. 18. 1599. in Vifitatione ordinaria R. P. D. Guil. Cotoni Exonienfis Epifcopi per Francifcum Godwynum ... Excudebat Edmund Bollifant. 1601.

Gosson, Stephen. The Trumpet of Warre. A Sermon preached at Paules Croffe the feuenth of Maie 1598. ... Printed at London by V. S. for I. O. dwelling in Paules churchyard at the figne of the Parot. [1598?]

Gravet, William. A sermon preached at Paules crosse on the XXV day of Iune Ann. Dom. 1587. intreating of the holy Scriptures, and of the vfe of the fame: ... Imprinted at London by Arnold Hatfield, and are to be fold in the little Old baily, in Eliots court. 1587.

Greenham, Richard. The works of the reuerend and faithfull feruant of Iesus Christ M. Richard Greenham, Minifter and

Preacher of the word of God: examined, corrected, and publiſhed, for the further building of all ſuch as loue the trueth, and deſire to know the power of godlines: ... Imprinted by Felix Kyngston for Robert Dexter, ... 1599. [7 sermons.] [Section beginning with sig. Dd 1 printed by R. Bradocke.]

........[Anr. ed.] ... F. Kingston for R. Iackson, 1599. [Not seen.]

........[Anr. ed.] ... The Second edition ... Felix Kingston, for Robert Dexter, ... 1599.

........[Anr. ed.] ... The Third Edition ... Felix Kyngston, for Robert Dexter, ... 1601.

........[Anr. ed.] ... F. Kingston for R. Iacson, 1601. [Not seen.]

........[Anr. ed.] ... the fourth and last edition ... Felix Kyngston, for Cuthbert Burbie, ... 1605. [Enlarged edition; contains 17 sermons.]

........A fruitful and godly sermon. Edinburgh, R. Waldegrave, 1595. [Not seen.]

........Two learned and godly sermons, Preached by that reuerende and zelous man M. Richard Greenham: on theſe partes of Scripture folowing. The firſt Sermon on this text. A good name is to be deſired aboue great riches, and louing fauour aboue ſiluer and golde. Pro. 22, 1. The ſecond Sermon on this text. Quench not the ſpirit. 1. Theſſa. 5, 19. ... Printed by Gabriel Simſon and William White, for William Iones, ... 1595.

Grindal, Edmund, *Abp.* A Sermon, at the Funeral Solemnitie of the moſt high and mighty Prince Ferdinandus, the late Emperour of moſt famous memorye, holden in the Cathedrall Churche of ſaint Paule in London, the third of October .1564. ... Imprinted at London by Iohn Day, ... [1564.]

........Concio Funebris in obitum Auguſtæ memoriæ Ferdinandi Cæſaris recens defuncti, in celeberrimo procerum ac magnatum conuentu Londini in Eccleſia Cathedrali D. Pauli habita. Octob. 3. Anno 1564. ... Ex Anglico, in Latinum conuerſa, Per Ioan. Foxum. Excuſum Londini, per Ioan. Dayum, ... 1564.

Hacket, Roger. A sermon needfull for theese times, wherein is shewed the insolencies of Naash King of Ammon, againſt the men of Iabeſh Gilead, and the ſuccors of Saule, and his people ſent for their relief. Preached at Paules Croſſe the 14 of Feb. 1590. . . . At Oxford. Printed by Ioseph Barnes Printer to the Uniuerſitie. 1591.

........A sermon preached at Newport-Paignell in the Countie of Buckingham. . . . Printed for Robert Wilſon, . . . 1628. [Preached in or before 1593.]

Hanmer, Meredith. The Baptizing of a Turke. A Sermon preached at the Hoſpitall of Saint Katherin, adioyning vnto her Maieſties Towre the 2. of October 1586. at the Baptizing of one Chinano a Turke, borne at Nigropontus: . . . Printed by Robert Walde-graue . . . [1586?]

Harris, Edmond. A sermon preached at Brocket Hall, before the Right Worſhipfull, Sir. Iohn Brocket, and other Gentlemen aſſembled for the trayning of Souldiers. Ianuary 2 and 3. . . . Printed by Thomas Orwin, for Iohn Daldern and William Haw. 1588.

........A sermon preached at Hitchin in the yeare of our Lord, 1587. the 17. day of Nouember, being the firſt day of the 29. yeare of the Queenes Maieſties reigne. . . . Printed at London by Iohn Morris & I. B. dwelling in S. Iohns ſtreete. 1590.

Harrison, William. Deaths aduantage little regarded, and the ſoules ſolace againſt ſorrow. Preached in two funerall Sermons at Childwal in Lancaſhire at the buriall of Mistres Katherin Brettergh the third of Iune. 1601. The one by William Harriſon, one of the Preachers appointed by her Maieſtie for the Countie Palatine of Lancaſter, the other by William Leygh, Bachelor of Diuinitie, and Pastor of Standiſh. Whereunto is annexed, the Chriſtian life and godly death of the ſaid Gentlewoman. The ſecond Edition, corrected and amended. . . . Imprinted by Felix Kyngston. 1602.

........[Anr. ed.] . . . Imprinted by Felix Kyngston. 1605.

Harward, Simon. The danger of Diſcontentment, Intreated of in a Sermon preached at Crowhurſt in Surrey the ninth of Iuly 1598. . . . Imprinted at London by W. W. for R. Iohnes. 1. Ian. 1599.

........Two godlie and learned Sermons preached at Mancheſter in Lancashire, before a great Audience, both of Honor and Worship. The firſt, containeth a reproofe of the ſubtill practifes of diffembling Neuters, and politique worldlings. The other, a charge and Instruction, for all vnlearned, negligent, and diffolute Minifters: And an exhortation to the common people, to feeke their amendment by prayer, vnto God. ... Imprinted at London by Iohn Charlewood, and Richard Ihones. 1582.

Hill, Adam. The crie of England. A Sermon preached at Paules Crofse in September 1593. ... & publifhed at the requeft of the then Lord Maior of the Citie of London, and others the Aldermen his brethren. ... Printed by Ed. Allde, for B. Norton. 1595.

Holland, Thomas. Oratio Sarisburiæ habita VIII. Id. Iun. cum reuerendus in Christo Pater Henricus permiffione divinâ Epifcopus Sarisburienfis gradum Doctoratus Theologiâ fufciperet, ex decreto Convocationis Oxonienfis. ... Oxoniæ, Excudebat Iofephus Barnefius. M.D.XCIX.

........Πανηγυϱις D. Elizabethæ, Dei gratiâ Angliæ, Franciæ, & Hiberniæ Reginæ. A sermon preached at Pauls in London the 17. of November Ann. Dom. 1599. the one and fortieth yeare of her Maiefties raigne, and augmented in thofe places wherein, for the fhortnes of the time, it could not there be delivered. Wherevnto is adioyned an Apologeticall difcourfe, whereby all fuch fclanderous Accufations are fully and faithfully confuted, wherewith the Honour of this Realme hath beene vncharitably traduced by fome of our adverfaries in foraine nations, and at home, for obferving the 17. of november yeerely in the forme of an Holy-day, and for the ioifull exercifes, and Courtly triumphes on that day in the honour of her Maieftie exhibited. ... At Oxford, Printed by Joseph Barnes, and are to be folde in Pauls Church-yard at the figne of the Bible. Ann. Dom. 1601.

The feconde Tome of Homelyes of fuch matters as were promifed and Intituled in the former part of Homelyes, fet out by the aucthoritie of the Quenes Maieftie: And to be read in euery paryfhe Churche agreablye. 1563. [Rychard Iugge, and Ihon Cawood.]

........[Anr. ed.] ... Iugge and Cawood, 1563.

........[Anr. ed.] ... Iugge and Cawood, 1563.

........[Anr. ed.] ... Iugge and Cawood, 1563.

........[Anr. ed] ... Iugge and Cawood, 1567.

........[Anr. ed.] ... Iugge and Cawood, 1570, The 23. of Iune.

........[Anr. ed.] ... Iugge and Cawood, 1571.

........[Anr. ed.] ... Richard Iugge, 1574.

........[Anr. ed.] ... Richard Iugge, 1577.

........[Anr. ed.] ... Chriſtopher Barker, 1582.

........[Anr. ed.] ... 1587.

........[Anr. ed.] ... Edward Allde, 1595.

........[Anr. ed.] Pregethau a oſodwych allan tiwy awdurdod i'w darllein ymhob Eglwys blwyf aphob capeler adailadaeth i'r bobl annyſwedig. Gwedi eu troi i'r iaith Gymeraeg drwy waith. Edward Iames. Robert Barker printiwr ... yn Llundain ... 1606.

[An Homilie againſt diſobedience and wylful rebellion.] Imprinted at London in Powles Churchyarde, by Richarde Iugge and Iohn Cawood, ... [1571?] [Title-page wanting.]

........[Anr. ed.] ... Imprinted at London in Powles Church yarde by Richard Iugge and Iohn Cawood, ... [1573?]

An Homyly, concerning the Iuſtice of God. [No title-page; runs from D1 to F4 of the 1563 Jugge and Cawood *Book of Common Prayer*.] [Not in S. T. C.]

A sermon, Or homelie, to Mooue Compaſsion towards the Poore and needie in theſe times: Vpon the wordes of the Apoſtle, Heb. 13. ver. 16. To doe good. &c. London Printed by Iohn Windet, for Andrew Maunſell. 1596. [Not in S. T. Cat.; Lambeth 30. 1. 22.]

The second sermon, or exhortation, Perſwading to Charitie, and Hoſpitalitie towards the Poore: Vpon the wordes of our Sauiour Luke. 14. verſe 13. 14. But when thou makeſt a feaſt, call the Poore. &c. Diuided into two partes. Set foorth by Authoritie. London Printed by I. Windet, for Andrew Maunſell. 1596. [Not in S. T. Cat.; Lambeth 78. C. 18.]

Three sermons, or homelies, to Mooue Compaſsion towards the Poore and needie in theſe times. Set foorth by Authoritie. London Printed by I. Windet for Andrew Maunſell. 1596.

A briefe homily, wherein the moſt comfortable and right vſe of the Lords Supper, is very plainly opened and deliuered, euen to the vnderſtanding of the vnlearned and ignorant. Made to be vſed throughout the Dioceſſe of Lincolne, before euerie celebration of the Lordes Supper, in all ſuch Churches and Pariſhes as haue not a ſufficient hable Preacher allowed vnder the hand and authentike ſeale of the Biſhop there, and to be read by the Miniſter of each ſuch place, ſo diſtinctly and in ſuch ſorte, that all which ſhal be then aſſembled, may well heare and marke the ſame. Imprinted at London for Ralph Newberie, . . . 1580.

Hooke, Christopher. The Child-birth or Womans Lecture. That is: A Lecture vpon Chap. 1. ver. 57, 58. of the holie Gospell according to Luke; very neceſſarie to bee read and knowne of all young married and teeming Women, and not vnprofitable for men of all ſortes. . . . Printed by Thomas Orwin, for Henry Hooke, and are to be ſold in Paules Churchyard, by Raphe Iackson, . . . 1590.

........A sermon preached in Paules Church in London: and publiſhed for the inſtruction and conſolation of all that are heauie harted, for the wofull time of God his generall viſitayion, both in the Citie and in the Countrie: and fit for the comfort of Gods Children at all times. . . . Imprinted at London by E. Allde. [1603.]

Hooker, Richard. A learned and comfortable sermon of the certaintie and perpetuitie of faith in the Elect; eſpecially of the Prophet Habakkuks faith. . . . At Oxford, Printed by Ioſeph Barnes, and are to be ſold by John Barnes dwelling neere Holborne Conduit. 1612.

........A learned discourse of iustification, workes, and how the foundation of faith is overthrowne. . . . At Oxford, Printed by Joſeph Barnes, and are to be ſold by John Barnes, dwelling neere Holborne Conduit. 1612.

........A learned sermon of the nature of pride, . . . At Oxford, Printed by Ioſeph Barnes, and are to be ſold by John Barnes dwelling neere Holborne Conduit. 1612.

........A remedie against sorrow and feare, delivered in a funerall Sermon, . . . At Oxford, Printed by Ioſeph Barnes, and are to be ſold by John Barnes dwelling neere Holborne Conduit. 1612.

........Two sermons vpon part of S. Judes epistle, . . . Printed at Oxford by Iofeph Barnes. Ann. Dom. 1614.

Horne, Robert, *Bp.* Life and Death. Foure sermons. The first two, of Our Preparation To Death; and Expectation Of Death. The last two, Of Peace, and the Iudgement After Death. Alfo points of inftruction for the ignorant, with an examination before our comming to the Lords Table, and a fhort direction for fpending of time well. . . . Printed by Iohn Pindley and Iohn Beale, for Francis Burton, . . . 1613.

Howson, John, *Bp.* A Sermon preached at Paules Croffe the 4. of December. 1597. Wherein is difcourfed, that all buying and felling of Spirituall promotion is vnlawfull. . . . Imprinted at London by Arn. Hatfield for Thomas Adams. 1597.

........[Anr. ed.] . . . Printed for Th. Adams. 1597.

........A Second Sermon, preached at Paules Croffe, the 21. of May, 1598. vpon the 21. of Math. the 12. and 13. verfes: Concluding a former Sermon Preached the 4. of December 1597. vpon the fame Text. . . . Imprinted at London by Arn. Hatfield for Thomas Adams, . . . 1598.

........A sermon preached at S. Maries in Oxford, the 17. day of November, 1602. in defence of the Festivities of the Church of England, and namely that of her Maiefties Coronation. . . . At Oxford, Printed by Jofeph Barnes, and are to be fold in Fleeteftreete at the figne of the Turkes head by Iohn Barnes. 1602.

........[Anr. ed.] . . . The fecond Imprefsion. . . . At Oxford, Printed by Jofeph Barnes, and are to be fold . . . by Iohn Barnes. 1603.

Hubbocke, William. An apologie of infants in a sermon: Prouing, by the reuealed will of God, that children preuented by death of their Baptifme, by Gods election, may be faued. By W. H. Preacher in the Tower of London. Seene and allowed by Authoritie. . . . Printed by the Widowe Orwin for Thomas Man. 1595.

Hudson, John. A sermon preached at Paules Croffe the IX of Februarie. Anno Dom. 1583. . . . Imprinted at London by Thomas Purfoote, and are to be fold at his Shop . . . 1584.

Humphrey, Laurence. Ad Illuftriffimam R. Elizabetham, . . .

oratio Woodſtockiæ habita. An. 1572. Auguſt .31. Londini apud Iohannem Dayum Typographum. An. Dom. 1572.

........[Anr. ed.] ... Iohannem Dayum ... 1572. [Contains additional material.] [Not in S. T. Cat.; Brit. Mus. C. 33. d. 1.]

........Oratio ad serenifs. Angliæ, Franciæ, & Hyberniæ Reginam Eliſabetham, in Aula Woodſtockienſi habita ... anno 1575. Septemb. 11. Londini, Typis Henrici Binnemani, impenſis Georgii Biſhop. 1575.

........A view of the Romish Hydra and monster, traison, against the Lords annointed: condemned by David, 1. Sam. 26. and nowe confuted in seuen sermons: To perſwade Obedience to Princes, Concord among our ſelues, and a generall Reformation and Repentaunce in all ſtates: ... At Oxford. Printed by Ioseph Barnes, and are to be ſolde in Paules Churchyearde at the ſigne of the Tygers head, 1588.

Humston, Robert. A sermon Preached at Reyſham in the Countie of Norff. the 22. of September, An. Do. 1588. And eftſoones at requeſt publiſhed ... Printed by Iohn Wolfe for Edward Aggas. 1589.

Hutchins, Edward. A sermon preached at S. Maries in Oxford vpon the feast of Epiphany concerning the true comfort of God his Church truly millitant and apologie of the ſame. Ianuary 6, 1589. ... Imprinted at Oxford by Ioſeph Barnes, and are to be ſold in Pauls Church yeard, at the ſigne of the Tygres head. [1589.]

........A sermon preached in S. Peters church at West-chester the XXV. of September, 1586. containing matter fit for the time: ... At Oxford, Printed by Ioseph Barnes, and are to be ſold in Pauls Church-yarde at the ſigne of the Tygers head. [1586.]

........A sermon preached in West-chester the VIII. of October, 1586. before the iudges and certain recusantes: Wherein the conditions of al heretiques, but eſpeciallie of ſtubborn and peruerting Papiſts, are diſcouered, & the duty of al magiſtrats concerning ſuch perſons, applied & opened . . . At Oxford printed by Ioseph Barnes, and are to be ſolde in Pauls Church-yard, at the ſigne of the Tygers head. [1586.]

Hutton, Matthew, *Abp.* A sermon Preached at Yorke, before the right Honorable, Henrie Earle of Huntington, Lorde Prefident of her Maiefties Councell eftablished in the North, and other noble men, and gentle men, at a general Communion there, the 23. of September in the eightienth yeare of her Maiefties raigne: ... Imprinted at London, for Richard Sergier. Anno. 1579. [Printed by Thomas Dawson.]

I., S. Certaine Godlie and learned Sermons. Made vpon thefe fixe following Parables of our Sauiour Chrift, declared in the Gofpell. 1. Of the vncleane fpirit. 2. Of the prodigall fonne. 3. Of the Rich man and Lazarus. 4. Of the wounded man. 5. Of the vnmercifull feruant. 6. Of the faithfull feruant. ... Printed by I. R. for R. B. and are to be folde in Paules Church-yard, at the figne of the Sunne. 1601. [6 sermons.]

Ingmethorpe, Thomas. A sermon vpon part of the second chapter of the firft epiftle of S. Iohn ... The fumme whereof is briefly comprifed in this Hexameter: ... He beares the bell away, that liues, as he doth faie. At Oxford, printed by Ioseph Barnes, Printer to the Vniverfitie. 1598.

........ [Anr. ed.] ... wherein the prefent State of the Papacie, is in part but vnpartially reprefented, and fhewed to be nothing leffe then Catholique, euen plaine Antichriftian. ... Printed by Thomas Creede. 1609.

Jackson, Thomas. Dauids Paftorall Poeme: or Sheepeheards Song. Seuen sermons, on the 23. Pfalme of Dauid, whereof the last was preached at Afhford in Kent, the day whereon our gracious King was there proclaimed. ... Printed by Thomas Purfoot, and are to bee fold by Edmund Weauer ... 1603.

James, William. A Sermon preached at Paules Crosse the IX of November, 1589. ... Imprinted at London by George Bishop and Ralph Newberie. 1590.

........ A sermon Preached before the Queenes Maieftie at Hampton Courte, the 19. of Februarie laft paft. ... Imprinted at London by Henry Bynneman. Anno Domini. 1578 Aprilis, 24.

Jewel, John, *Bp.* The works of the very learned and Reuerend Father in God Iohn Iewell, not long fince Bifhop of Sarisburie. Newly fet forth with fome amendment of diuers quotations: and a brief discourfe of his life. ... Printed by Iohn

Norton, Printer to the Kings moſt excellent Maieſtie. 1609. [13 Elizabethan sermons.]

........Certaine Sermons preached before the Queenes Maiſtie, and at Paules croſſe, ... Whereunto is added a ſhort treatiſe of the Sacraments, gathered out of other of his ſermons made vpon that matter, in his cathedrall Church at Saliſburie. Imprinted at London, by Chriſtopher Barker, Printer to the Queenes moſt excellent Maieſtie. 1583. [5 sermons.]

........[Anr. ed.] ... [Imprinted . . . by Chriſtopher Barker, . . . 1583.] [Title-page lacking.]

........[Anr. issue] ... [No place, no date.] [Not seen.]

........[Anr. ed.] ... Imprinted at London for William Leake, . . . 1603.

........The copie of a Sermon pronounced by the Byſhop of Saliſburie at Paules Croſſe the ſecond Sondaye before Eſter in the yere of our Lord .1560. whervpon D. Cole firſt ſought occaſion to encounter, ſhortly ſet forthe as nere as the authour could call it to remembraunce, without any alteration or addition. ... [Printed by John Day, 1560.]

........Seuen godly sermons; neuer before imprinted. G. Bishop, 1607. [Not seen.]

........A viewe of a seditious Bul ſent into England, from Pius Quintus Biſhop of Rome, Anno. 1569. Taken by the reuerend Father in God, Iohn Iewel, late Biſhop of Salisburie. Whereunto is added A ſhort Treatise of the holy Scriptures. Both which he deliuered in diuers Sermons in his Cathedral Church of Salisburie, Anno. 1570. . . . Printed by R. Newberie, & H. Bynneman. Anno. 1582. [1 sermon and 1 treatise summing up several sermons.]

Jones, Philip. Certaine Sermons preached of late at Ciceter, in the countie of Glocester, vpon a portion of the firſt Chapter of the Epiſtle of Iames: wherein the two ſeueral ſtates, of the riche and poore man are compared and examined, the differences in quality, and duety betwixt them ſhewed, both directed to ſuch Chriſtian parts and offices, as the ſufficiencie of the one may, and ought to performe, and the wants of the other do neceſſarily require. Penned at the earneſt requeſts of diuers well affected Inhabitantes of the place: and now publiſhed as well for the vſe of others, as for the further profit of that particular congregation . . . Allowed by authoritie. Imprinted at London by T. D. for Thomas Butter 1588.

Keltridge, John. The Exposition, and Readynges of Iohn Keltridge: . . . Vpon the wordes of our Sauiour Chriſte, that be written in the xi of Luke. . . . Imprinted at London, by William How, for Abraham Veale. 1578. [Contains a sermon on I Tim. 3:1. preached at Fulham in 1577. page 219.]

........Two godlie and learned Sermons, appointed, and Preached, before the Jeſuites, Seminaries, and other adverſaries to the Goſpell of Chriſt in the Tower of London. In which, were confuted to their faces, the moſte principall and cheefe poincts of their Romiſh and Whoariſh religion: And all ſuch Articles as they defend, contrarie to the woord of God, were layed open and ripped vp vnto them. In Maye, 7. and 21. Anno. 1581. . . . Imprinted at London by Richard Ihones, . . . [1581.]

Kethe, William. A sermon made at Blanford Forũ, in the Countie of Dorſet on Wenſday the 17. of Ianuarie laſt paſt at the Seſſion holden there, before the honorable and the worſhyppefull of that Shyre, . . . Printed by Iohn Daye, . . . 1571.

King, John, *Bp.* Lectures vpon Ionas, deliuered at Yorke in the yeare of our Lorde 1594. . . . Printed at Oxford, by Joseph Barnes, and are to be ſolde in Paules Church-yarde at the ſigne of the Bible. 1597. [48 lectures and 2 sermons.]

........[Anr. ed.] . . . Printed at Oxford, by Ioseph Barnes, and are to be ſolde in Paules Church-yarde at the ſigne of the Bible. 1599.

........[Anr. ed.] . . . Printed at Oxford, by Ioseph Barnes, and are to be ſolde in Paules Church-yarde at the ſigne of the Bible. 1600.

Knewstub, John. A Confutation of Monſtrous and horrible hereſies, taught by H. N. and embraced of a number, who call themſelues the Familie of Loue. . . . Seene and allowed, according to the Queenes Maieſties Iniunctions. Imprinted . . . by Thomas Dawſon, for Richard Sergier. 1579. [Contains (sig. P1 to S4) a sermon preached at Pauls Cross on Good Friday, 1576.]

........Lectures of Iohn Knewſtub, vpon the twentieth Chapter of

Exodus, and certeine other places of Scripture. Seene and allowed according to the Queenes Maieſties Iniunctions. Imprinted by Lucas Harriſon. Anno. 1577. [17 lectures.]

........[Anr. ed.] ... Imprinted by Lucas Harriſon. Anno. 1578.

........[Anr. ed.] ... Imprinted for Thomas Woodcocke. Anno. 1579.

........[Anr. ed.] ... Imprinted for Thomas Woodcocke. Anno. 1584.

........A Sermon preached at Paules Croſſe the Fryday before Eaſter, commonly called good Friday, in the yeere of our Lorde .1579. ... Printed ... by Thomas Dawſon for Richard Sergier. 1579.

Knox, John. A notable and Comfortable expoſition of M. Iohn Knoxes, vpon the fourth of Mathew, concerning the tentations of Chriſt: Firſt had in the publique Church, and then afterwards written for the comfort of certaine priuate friends, but now publiſhed in print for the benefite of all that feare God. ... Printed by Robert Walde-graue, for Thomas Man, ... [1583.]

........A sermon preached ... in the Publique audience of the Church of Edenbrough, within the Realme of Scotland, vpon Sonday, the 19. of August .1565. For the which the ſaid Iohn Knoxe was inhibite preaching for a ſeaſon. 1. Timoth. 4. The time is come that men can not abyde the Sermon of veritie nor holſome doctrine. To this is adioyned an exhortation vnto all the faythfull within the ſayde Realme, for the reliefe of ſuche as faythfully trauayle in the preaching of Gods worde. Written by the ſame Iohn Knoxe, at the commaundement of the ministerie aforeſayd. Imprinted Anno. 1566.

Leake, Richard. Foure sermons, preached and publikely taught by Richard Leake, Preacher of the word of God at Killington, within the Baronie of Kendall and Countie of Weſtmerland: immediately after the great viſitation of the peſtilence in the foreſayd Countie. ... Imprinted by Felix Kingston, for Thomas Man. 1599.

Lewes, R. A sermon preached at Paules Croſſe, ... concerning Iſaac his Testament, diſpoſed by the Lord to Iacobs comfort, though it were intended to Eſau by his father; ſhewing that the counſel of God ſhal ſtand, albeit the whole worlde withſtande it. At Oxford, Printed by Ioseph Barnes, Printer to that famous Vniuerſitie. M.D.XCIIII.

Leygh, William. [See above, under William Harrison, *Deaths Aduantage.*]

Madoxe, Richard. A Learned and a Godly Sermon, to be read of all men, but eſpecially for all Marryners, Captaynes, and Paſſengers, which trauell the Seas, preached . . . at Waymouth and Melcombe regis, a Porte in the Countie of Dorſett, the 3. day of October, in the yeere of our Lord. 1581. . . . Printed by I. Charlwood. [1581.]

Marbury, Francis. A fruitful sermon necessary for the time, preached at the Spittle vpon the Tueſday in Eaſter weeke laſt, by Frauncis Marbury. Publiſhed by direction of Authoritie. Printed at London by P. Short, . . . 1602.

........A sermon preached at Paules Crosse the 13. of Iune, 1602. . . . Printed by Peter Short, and are to be ſold in Paules Church-yard at the ſigne of the Swanne. 1602.

Massie, William. A sermon preached at Trafford in Lancashire at the mariage of a daughter of the right Worſhipfull Sir Edmond Trafforde Knight, the 6. of September Anno. 1586. . . . At Oxford. Printed by Ioseph Barnes, and are to be ſolde in Paules Church-yard at the ſigne of the Tigres head, 1586.

Mosse, Miles. The arraignment and conuiction of vsurie. That is, The iniquitie, and vnlawfulness of vſurie, diſplayed in ſixe Sermons, preached at Saint Edmunds Burie in Suffolke, vpon Prouerb .28. 8. . . . Seene and allowed by authoritie. The especiall contents of this booke, are declared in the page next before the treatiſe it ſelfe. Reade all, or cenſure none. . . . Printed by the widdow Orwin, for Thomas Man. 1595.

Nicholson, Samuel. A Sermon, called Gods New-yeeres-guift ſent vnto England. Conteined in these wordes. [John 3:16] . . . Printed by W. White, and are to be ſold by Y. Iames . . . 1602.

........[Anr. ed.] Gods new-yeeres gift ſent vnto England: Or, The ſumme of the Goſpell, contayned in theſe wordes; God ſo loued the world, that he hath giuen his onely begotten Sonne, that whoſoeuer beleeueth in him, ſhould not periſh, but ſhould haue life euerlaſting. John 3. 16. The firſt part. . . . Imprinted at London, by Simon Stafford, . . . 1602.

Overton, William, *Bp.* A Godlye and pithie Exhortation, made to the Iuſtices of Suſſex, and the whole Countie, aſſembled togither, at the generall Aſsiſes. By William Ouerton, Doctor of Diuinitie, and one of the Queenes Maieſties Iuſtices appoynted for the peace within the ſame Countie. ... Printed by R. Newbery and H. Bynneman. [1580.]

........Oratio doctissima et grauissima, a reuerendo in Chriſto Patre Guilielmo Ouertono Lichfieldienſi Epiſcopo habita, in domo ibidem Capitulari, ad Præbendarios, & reliquum Clerum in Viſitatione Eccleſiæ ſuæ Cathedralis congregatum, Ann. Dom. 1600. Oxoniæ, Excudebat Ioſephus Barneſius. 1601.

Pagit, Eusebius. A godlie and fruitefull Sermon, made vpon the 20. & 21. verſes of the 14 Chapter of the booke of Geneſis: Wherein there is taught, what prouiſion ought to be made for the myniſter. Very neceſſary to be learned of all Chriſtians. ... Imprinted by Iohn Wolfe, for Thomas Man, ... 1583.

........[Anr. ed.] [Anon.] [No place, no printer, no date.] [1584?]

........[Anr. ed.] ... By E. P. ... [No place, no printer, no date.] [1585?]

........A godly sermon: Preached at Detford in Kent, on Monday the ix of Iune, in Anno. 1572. ... Printed for Thomas Man. An. 1586.

Perkins, William. Lectures vpon the three first chapters of the Reuelation: Preached in Cambridge Anno. Dom. 1595. ... and now publiſhed for the benebite [sic] of this Church, by Robert Hill Bachelor in Diuinitie. To which is added an excellent Sermon, penned at the requeſt of that noble and wiſe Councellor, Ambrose, Earle of Warwicke: in which is proued that Rome is Babylon, and that Babylon is fallen. ... Printed by Richard Field for Cuthbert Burbie, ... 1604. [Not divided into separate lectures.]

........[Anr. ed.] ... A. Islip for C. Burbie, 1606. [Not seen.]

........[Anr. ed.] ... A. Islip for C. Burbie. 1607. [Not seen.]

Peters fall. A godlie sermon: Vpon the Historie of Peters denying Christ, preached before the Queenes moſt excellent Maiestie. In which Sermon we haue to confider of thefe three Circumftances: firft of the person, fecondly of the euill wherein he fell, and thirdly of the occafion. Wherein euery faithfull Chriftian may fee before his eyes, the patterne of vnfeyned repentance. Whereby we may take heede of the falling into finne againe. Imprinted at London for Iohn Perin, ... 1585.

Phillips, George. Fiue godly and learned sermons. J. Roberts, 1594. [Not seen.]

........Gods Generall Summons to his laft Parliament. ... Printed for William Leake, ... 1595. [There is no indication that this is or is not a sermon.]

........[Anr. ed.] ... Printed for William Leake, ... 1597.

Pigge, Oliver. A comfortable treatife vpon the latter part of the fourth chapiter of the firft Epiftle of Saint Peter, from the twelfe verfe to the ende. ... Seene and alowed. ... Printed by Robert Walde-graue, for Iohn Harifon the yonger, and Thomas Man. 1582. [2 sermons preached at Burie in Suffolk.]

Pinner, Charles. A sermon, vpon the wordes of Paul the Apoftle vnto Timothie, Epift. 1. Chap. 4. verf. 8. Preached at Litlecot, in the Chappel of the Right Honourable, Sir Iohn Pompham, Knight, Lord chief Iuftice of England, before his honourable Lordefhippe, and to the affemblie there, the 17. of Iulie, 1597. ... Printed at Oxford by Iofeph Barnes, and are to be folde in Paules Church-yard at the figne of the Bible. 1597.

........[A sermon preached at Marlbrough, on 1. Tim. 4: 6. Preached before October 20, 1596.] [Title-page wanting.]

........Two sermons, on thefe wordes of Peter the Apoftle: Honour all men: Loue brotherly felowfhip. Epift. 1. chap. 2. verf. 17. Preached at Marlebrough the feuenth of Nouember, and fifth of Ianuarie 1575, ... Printed by Thomas Creede. 1597. [Preached in 1595, not 1575.]

Playfere, Thomas. The whole sermons of That Eloquent Diuine, of Famous Memory; Thomas Playfere, ... Gathered into one vollume, the Titles thereof are named in the next Page. ... Printed by T. S. for Matthew Law, ... 1623. [14 sermons; 7 Elizabethan.]

........Ten sermons preached By that eloquent Divine of famous memorie, ... Printed by Cantrell Legge, Printer to the Vniverſitie of Cambridge. 1610.

........Hearts delight. A sermon preached At Pauls croſſe in London in Eaſter terme. 1593. ... Printed by Iohn Legat, Printer to the Vniuerſitie of Cambridge. 1603. And are to be ſold in Pauls Churchyard at the ſigne of the Crowne by Simon Waterſon.

........A most excellent and heauenly sermon: Vpon the 23. Chapter of the Goſpell of Saint Luke. The Text. Luke 23. 28. Weepe not for me, but weepe for your ſelues. ... Printed, for Andrew Wiſe. 1595.

........The meane in mourning. A Sermon preached at Saint Maryes Spittle in London on Tueſday in Easter weeke. 1595. ... Printed by the Widow Orwin for Andrew Wiſe, ... 1596.

........[Anr. ed.] ... Printed by Iames Roberts for Andrew Wiſe, ... 1597.

........[Anr. ed.] ... Printed by Felix Kyngston for Matthew Law, ... 1607.

........The pathway to perfection. A Sermon preached at Saint Maryes Spittle in London on Wedneſday in Eaſter weeke. Printed by the Widow Orwin for Andrew Wiſe, ... 1596.

........[Anr. ed.] ... Printed by Iames Roberts for Andrew Wiſe, ... 1597.

........[Anr. ed.] ... Printed by Felix Kyngston for Matthew Law, ... 1607.

........The power of praier. A sermon preached in the Cathedrall Church of Exeter in Auguſt. 1596. ... Printed by Iohn Legat, Printer to the Vniuerſitie of Cambridge. 1603. And are to be ſold by Simon Waterſon.

........Sufficit. Sive, de Miſericordia dei in Differenda ira; Concio ad clerum Cantabrigienſem habita, in Templo B. Mariæ. Anno 1603. Ianuar. 12. ... Impenſis Thomæ Chard, & venundantur in officina Nathanaelis Fosbrooke. Anno. 1607. April. 3.

Pont, Robert. Against sacrilege, three sermons. Edinburgh, Robert Waldegrave, 1599. [Not seen.]

Porder, Richard. A Sermon of gods fearefull threatnings for

Idolatrye, mixing of religion, retayning of Idolatrous remnaunts, and other wickedneſſe: with a Treatiſe againſt Uſurie. Preached in Paules Churche the xv. daye of Maye. 1570. being Monday in Whitſon weeke. Written and dedicated to the Magiſtrates and all the Citizens of London: with a briefe table to finde out the principall matters contayned therin: by Richard Porder. Seene and allowed according to the Queenes Iniunctions. ... Imprinted by Henry Denham. [1570.]

Presse, Symon. A sermon preached at Eggington, in the County of Darby, concerning the right vſe of things indifferent, the 3. Day of Auguſt. 1596. ... Printed at Oxford by Ioſeph Barnes, and are to bee ſolde in Paules Church-yard at the ſigne of the Bible. 1597.

Price, Henry. The eagles flight Or Six principall notes, or ſure markes for euery true Christian, to ſoare vp to the euerlaſting neſt of Gods Eternal kingdome. As it was deliuered in a moſt godly and fruitfull Sermon at Paules Croſſe. ... Imprinted at London by Richard Bradocke for Iohn Buſbie, ... 1599.

Prime, John. The consolations of Dauid, breefly applied to Queene Elizabeth: In a Sermon preached at Oxford the 17. of Nouember. ... Imprinted at Oxford by Joſeph Barnes, and are to be ſold in Paules Church-yeard, at the ſigne of the Tygres head, 1588.

........A sermon briefly comparing the estate of King Salomon and his Subiectes togither with the condition of Queene Elizabeth and her people. Preached in Sainct Maries in Oxford the 17 of Nouember, and now printed with ſome ſmall alteration, ... 1585. Imprinted at Oxford by Ioſeph Barnes Printer to the Vniuerſitie. 1585.

Rainolds, John. A sermon vpon part of the eighteenth Psalm: Preached to the publik aſſemblie of Scholers in the Vniuerſitie of Oxford the laſt day of Auguſt, 1586. ... Vpon occaſion of their meeting to giue thanks to God for the late detection and apprehenſion of Traitours, who wickedlie conſpired againſt the Queenes Maieſtie and the ſtate of the Realme. Psalm 20. 6. Now knowe I that the Lord doth ſaue his annointed, doth heare him out of his holie heauens, by excellent ſtrength, the ſafegard of his right hand. At Oxford, Printed by Ioseph Barnes, Printer to the Vniuerſitie, 1586.

........A Sermon vpon part of the Propheſie of Obadiah: Touching the deſtruction, as of Idumæans, so of Papiſts; and means whereby it muſt be wrought: Preached at Saint Maries in Oxford by Iohn Rainoldes, on the 28. of October laſt. 1584. Printed .1584. [Printed by Thomas Dawson.]

Roberts, Hugh. The day of hearing: Or, six lectures vpon the latter part of the thirde Chapter of the Epiſtle to the Hebrewes: of the time and meanes that God hath appointed for men to come to the knowledge of his truth, that they may be ſaved from his wrath. The ſummary pointes of every one of which Lectures are ſet downe immediately after the epiſtle dedicatory. Herevnto is adioyned a Sermon againſt fleſhly luſts, & againſt certaine miſchievous May-games which are the fruit thereof. ... Printed at Oxford by Ioſeph Barnes, and are to be ſold in Paules church-yard, at the ſigne of the Bible. 1600. [7 sermons.]

Rogers, Thomas. A sermon vpon the 6. 7. and 8. Verſes of the 12. Chapter of S. Pauls Epiſtle vnto the Romanes; Made to the Confutation of ſo much of another Sermon, entituled, A Frutful Sermon &c. as concerneth both the depriuation of the præſent gouerment, and the perpetual, and vniforme regiment of our Church By certaine their deſcribed Officers to be in euerie particular Pariſh through-out al her Maiesties Dominions; More fullie penned, than could by mouth be expreſſed, the tyme limitted to the ſpeaker being verie ſhort. Publiſhed at the request of certaine friends by Thomas Rogers. Allowed by auctoritie. ... Printed by Iohn Windet, 13. April. 1590.

Rollock, Robert. Certaine sermons vpon seuerall places of the Epiſtles of Paul. ... Edinburgh Printed by Henrie Charteris. 1599. Cum Priuilegio Regali. [11 sermons.]

........Certain sermons, vpon seuerall Texts of Scripture: ... Whereof the firſt eleuen were before publiſhed, and the remnant seuen, are newly adjoyned thereunto. Imprinted at Edinburgh, by Andro Hart. 1616. [18 sermons.]

........Fiue and twentie lectures, vpon the last sermon and conference of our Lord Iesus Christ, With his Difciples immediately before his Pafsion: Contained in the fourteenth, fifteenth, and fixteenth Chapters of the Gospel of Sainct Iohn. As alfo vpon that most excellent Prayer, contained in the feuenteenth Chap. of the fame Gofpel. ... Edinburgh, Printed by Andro Hart, 1619.

........Lectures vpon the first and second Epistles of Paul to the Thessalonians: ... Edinburgh Printed by Robert Charteris Printer to the Kings moft excellent Majeftie. An. Dom. M.D.C.VI. Cum Priuilegio Regiæ Majeftatis. [41 lectures.]

........Lectures vpon the Epistle of Paul to the Colossians. ... Imprinted by Felix Kyngston, ... 1603. [41 lectures.]

........Lectures, vpon the history of the Passion, Resurrection, and Ascension of our Lord Iesus Christ. Beginning at the eighteenth Chapter of the Gofpell, according to S. Iohn, and from the 16. verfe of the 19. Chapter thereof, containing a perfect Harmonie of all the foure Euangelifts, for the better vnderftanding of all the Circumftances of the Lords death, and Refurrection. ... Edinburgh, Printed by Andro Hart. Anno 1616. [56 lectures.]

Rudd, Anthony, *Bp*. A sermon preached at Richmond before Queene Elizabeth of famous memorie, vpon the 28. of March, 1596. ... Printed for Thomas Man. 1603.

S., D. A Godly learned and fruitfull Sermon. Made vpon the fourteenth of Iohn in which is plainely fet foorth the true looue of Chrift, the markes whereby the Children of God are knowen and the commoditie which that looue bringeth. By D. S. 1584. ... Printed for Yarath Iames, and Thomas Lawe and, are to be folde in newgate market ouer againft Chrifte Chvrch gate. [1584.]

S., L. Resurgendum A notable sermon concerning the resurrection, preached not long fince at the Court, by L. S. ... Printed by Iohn Wolfe. 1593.

Sandys, Edwin, *Abp*. Sermons Made by the moft reuerende Father in God, Edwin, Archbifhop of Yorke, Primate of England and Metropolitane. ... Printed by Henrie Midleton, for Thomas Charde. 1585. [22 sermons.]

Scott, Thomas. A godlie Sermon of repentaunce and amendment of life, togeather with the accompt which we muſt render at the day of iudgement. Preached at the Rolles Church in London the ſecond of Maye, and taken out of the fifth Chapter of Saint Paule his Epiſtle to the Corrinthians. ... Printed by Thomas Purfoote, and are to be ſold at his ſhop, ... 1585.

A godlye sermon: Preached before the Queenes moſt excellent Maieſtie, vpon the 17, 18, 19. verſes of the 16. Chapter of S. Mathew: Wherein is contained the concluſion of a Dialogue between Chriſt and his Diſciples: Shewing breefely that the authoritie which the Pope of Rome doth challenge to himſelfe, is vnlawfully vſurped. Very neceſſarie for theſe perilous times wherein the ſimple may perceiue their intollerable impietie, vſurping that office and action which euer appertayned vnto Chriſt only. Publiſhed at the request of ſundry godly and well diſpoſed perſons. Printed at London by Iohn Windet for Iohn Perin, ... 1585.

A sermon preached before the Queenes Maieſtie, the ſecond of March, An 1575. ... Imprinted at London, by Rycharde Watkins. Cum Priuilegio. [1575.]

A Verie fruitful Sermon, neceſſary to be read of all Chriſtians, concerning Gods euerlaſting Predeſtination, Election, and Reprobation: made by a Godly Miniſter vpon the 25. chap. of Geneſis. ver. 23. Now publiſhed for the edifying of Chriſt his Church. At London Printed by Roger Warde for Thomas Man. Anno Domini. 1583.

Shelford, Robert. Lectures Or Readings vpon the 6. verſe of the 22. chapter of Prouerbs, concerning the vertuous education of Youth: A treatiſe very neceſſarie for all parents in this corrupt and declining age of the world. At London, Printed by Felix Kingston for Thomas Man. 1602. [6 lectures?]

........[Anr. ed.] ... F. Kyngston for T. Man. 1606. [Not seen.]

Shutt, Christopher. A verie godlie and neceſſary Sermon preached before the yong Counteſſe of Comberland in the North, the 24. of Nouember, 1577. ... Imprinted at London by Chriſtopher Barker, Printer to the Queenes Maieſtie. [1578.]

Smith, Henry. The affinitie of the faithfull: Being a verie Godlie and fruitfull Sermon, made vpon part of the eight Chapter of the Gospel of Saint Luke. ... Printed by William Hoskins and Henrie Chettle, for Nicholas Ling, and Iohn Busbie. 1591.

........[Anr. ed.] ... Nowe the ſecond time Imprinted, corrected, and augmented according to the Coppie by Characterie, as he preached it. ... Printed for Nicholas Ling by Iohn Busbie. 1591.

........The Chriſtians Sacrifice. Seene and allowed. ... Printed by Thomas Orwin, for Thomas Man. 1589.

........[Anr. ed.] ... Printed for Thomas Man. Anno. 1591.

........The examination of vsury, in two Sermons. Taken by Characterie, and after examined. Imprinted at London by R. Field for Thomas Man, ... 1591.

........[Anr. ed.] ... Imprinted at London by Thomas Orwin for Thomas Man, ... 1591.

........The fall of King Nabuchadnezzer. Dan. 4. 28. 29. 30. ... Printed by Thomas Scarlet, 1591.

........The first sermon of Noahs drunkennes. A glasse wherein all drunkards may behold their beaſtlineſſe. Noah alſo began to be an husbandman and planted a vineyard, and he dranke of the wine and was drunken, and was vncouered in the middeſt of his tent. Gen. 9.20. ... Imprinted at London by William Kearney ... 1591.

........A fruitfull sermon, Vpon part of the 5. Chapter of the firſt Epiſtle of Saint Paul to the Theſſalonians, ... Which Sermon being taken by Characterie, is now publiſhed for the benefite of the faithfull. ... Printed for Nicholas Ling. 1591. [Printed by William Hoskins, Henry Chettle, and John Danter.]

........[Anr. ed.] ... Printed for the widdowe Broome. 1591.

........Iacobs ladder, or the high way to heauen: Being the laſt Sermon that Maſter Henry Smith made. And now publiſhed, not (as many forged things haue beene in his name) to deceiue the Chriſtian Reader, but to inſtruct and prepare him with oyle in his lampe, ioyfully to meete the Lord Ieſus in his ſecond comming ... Printed by the widdow Orwin, for Thomas Man. 1595.

........The lawiers Question. The Anſwere to the Lawiers Queſtion. The Cenſure of Chriſt vpon the Anſwere. ... Printed for Thomas Goſſon: ... [1595.] [3 sermons.]

........The magistrates scripture, Which treateth of their election, excellencie, qualities, dutie, and end: with two godly prayers annexed thereunto. . . . Printed by William Kearney, . . . 1590.

........[Anr. ed.] ... Imprinted by William Kearney, ... 1591.

........Maries choise. With prayers written by the ſame Author. ... Printed by T. Scarlet, for Cuthbert Burby. 1592.

........The poore-mans teares. Opened in a Sermon preched by Henrie Smith. Treating of Almes deeds; and releeuing the poore ... Printed by Iohn Wolfe, & are to be ſold by William Wright. 1592. [4 sermons: Poor mans tears, Harmony from heaven, Memento for Magistrates, and The wedding garment.]

........The preachers Proclamacion. Diſcourſing the vanity of all earthly things, and proouing that there is no contentation to a Chriſtian minde, but onely in the feare of God. ... Imprinted at London by William Kearney ... 1591.

........A Preparatiue to Mariage. The ſumme whereof was ſpoken at a Contract, and inlarged after. Whereunto is annexed a Treatiſe of the Lords Supper, and another of Vſurie. ... Imprinted at London by Thomas Orwin for Thomas Man, ... 1591. [5 sermons.]

........[Anr. ed.] ... Newly corrected and augmented by the Author. Imprinted at London by R. Field for Thomas Man, ... 1591. [5 sermons.]

........[Anr. ed.] ... Printed by I. Charlewood for Thomas Man, ... 1591. [5 sermons and Smith's death-bed speech.]

........The Pride of King Nabuchadnezzar. Dan. 4. 26. 27. ... Printed by Thomas Scarlet. 1591.

........[Anr. ed.] ... Printed by Thomas Scarlet, and are to be ſold by William Wright. 1591.

........The Reſtitution of King Nabuchadnezzer. Dan. 4. Verſes. 31. 32. 33. 34. ... Printed by Thomas Scarlet. 1591. [Sold by William Wright.]

........[Anr. ed.] ... Printed by Thomas Scarlet. 1591. [Sold by

William Wright.] [This edition differs from the above in that this edition is paged, while the other is not.]

........Satans compassing the earth. ... Imprinted by Thomas Scarlet. 1592.

........A Sermon of the benefite of Contentation. ... Taken by Characterie. ... Printed by Roger Ward, for Iohn Proctor, ... 1590.

........[Anr. ed.] The benefite of Contentation. Taken by Characterie, and examined after. ... Printed by Roger Ward, for Iohn Proctor, ... 1590.

........[Anr. ed.] ... Printed by Abell Ieffes for Roger Ward, 1590.

........[Anr. ed.] ... Newly examined and corrected by the Author. ... Printed by Abell Ieffes. 1591.

........The sinfull mans search: or seeking of God. Preached by Henrie Smith, and publiſhed according to a true corrected Copie, ſent by the Author to an Honorable Ladie. ... Printed for Cuthbert Burby. 1592.

........[Anr. ed.] ... Printed by T. S. for Cuthbert Burby. 1594.

........[Anr. ed.] ... Imprinted by Thomas Scarlet for Cuthbert Burby. 1594. [2 sermons; contains *Maries Choice.*]

........[Anr. ed.] ... Printed for Cuthbert Burby. [1596?]

........The sinners confeſsion. ... printed for William Leake, ... 1594.

........The sinners conuerſion. ... printed for William Leake, ... 1594.

........A Treatiſe of the Lords Supper, in two Sermons. Imprinted at London by Thomas Orwin for Thomas Man, ... 1591. [Not in S. T. Cat.; Bodl. 1. C. 405.]

........[Anr. ed.] ... Imprinted at London by R. Field for Thomas Man, ... 1591. [Misdated 1596 in S. T. Cat.]

........The trumpet of the Soule, ſounding to Iudgement. ... Printed for Iohn Perrin, ... 1591.

........[Anr. ed.] ... Printed for John Perrin, 1592. [Not seen.]

........[Anr. ed.] ... A. Jeffes 1592. [Not seen.]

........[Anr. ed.] ... Printed for the widdow Perrin, ... Anno. 1593.

........The wedding Garment. Rom. 13. 14. Put yee on the Lorde Ieſus Chriſt. ... Printed for W. Wright. 1590.

........[Anr. ed.] ... Printed for William Wright. [1590?]

........[Anr. ed.] ... At London printed. 1591.

........[Anr. ed.] ... At London printed. 1591. [Not in S. T. Cat. A different set-up of type. Brit. Mus. 4474. a. 26.]

[Collections of Thomas Man.]

........Seuen godly and learned sermons vpon seuen diuers Textes of Scripture, containing necessary and profitable doctrine, as well for the reformation of our liues as for the comfort of troubled confciences in all diftreffes. ... Perufed by the Author before his death. Imprinted at London by R. Field for Thomas Man, ... 1591.

........Thirteene sermons vpon seuerall Textes of Scripture. Containing necessarie and profitable doctrine, as well for the reformation of our liues, as for the comfort of troubled confciences in all diftreffes. ... Printed for Thomas Man, ... 1592.

........The sermons of master Henrie Smith, gathered into one volume. Printed according to his corrected Copies in his life time. ... Printed by Thomas Orwin for Thomas Man, ... 1592. [37 sermons.]

........[Anr. ed.] ... Printed by Richard Field for Thomas Man, 1593. [37 sermons.]

........[Anr. ed.] ... Printed by Peter Short for Thomas Man, ... 1594. [36 sermons.]

........[Anr. ed.] ... Printed by the Widdow Orwin, for Thomas Man, ... 1595. [Title-page wanting.]

........[Anr. ed.] ... Printed by Felix Kingston, for Thomas Man, ... 1597.

........[Anr. ed.] ... Imprinted by Felix Kingfton for Thomas Man. 1599.

........[Anr. ed.] ... Imprinted by Felix Kyngfton for Thomas Man, 1601.

........[Anr. ed.] ... Whereunto is added, Gods arrow againft Atheifts. ... Imprinted by Felix Kyngston, for Thomas Man. 1604.

........[Anr. ed.] ... Imprinted by Felix Kyngston, for Thomas Man, ... 1607. [42 sermons.]

........[Anr. ed.] ... Imprinted by Felix Kyngston, for Thomas Man, ... 1609. [41 sermons.]

[Collections of Ling and Smethwick.]

........Three sermons. J. Roberts for N. Ling, 1599. [Not seen.]

........Three Sermons ... I. The Benefit of Contentation. II. The Affinitie of the faithfull. III. The loſt Sheepe is found. ... Printed by Valentine Simmes, for Nicholas Ling, ... 1601.

........[Anr. ed.] ... Imprinted by F. K. for Nicholas Ling, ... 1604.

........[Anr. ed.] ... Imprinted by F. K. for Nicholas Ling, ... 1607.

........[Anr. ed.] ... Printed for Iohn Smethwicke, ... 1609.

[Collections of Cuthbert Burby.]

........Foure sermons preached by Master Henry Smith. And publiſhed by a more perfect copie than heretofore. ... Printed by P. S. for Cutbert Burby. 1599. [6 sermons.]

........[Anr. ed.] ... Printed by S. S. for Cutbert Burby. 1602.

........[Anr. ed.] ... T. C. for C. Burby, 1605. [Not seen.]

........[Anr. ed.] ... Printed by T. D. for Cuthbert Burby. 1607.

........[Anr. ed.] ... Printed by T. D. for Elizabeth Burby. 1609. [Not in S. T. Cat.; Brit. Mus. 4454. b. 25.]

........Two sermons of Ionahs Puniſhment, ... And publiſhed by a more perfect Copie then heretofore. ... Printed by S. S. for Cutbert Burby. 1602.

........[Anr. ed.] ... Printed by T. C. for Cutbert Burby. 1605.

........[Anr. ed.] ... Printed by T. D. for Cuthbert Burby. 1607.

........[Anr. ed.] ... Printed by T. D. for Elizabeth Burby. 1609.

[Collections of William Leake.]

........Foure sermons ... Printed by I. R. for William Leake, ... 1602. [The Leake collections of *Foure Sermons* consist of 2 sermons on the Song of Simeon, *The Calling of Ionah,* and *The Rebellion of Ionah.*]

........[Anr. ed.] ... Printed for William Leake, ... 1608.

........[Anr. ed.] ... Printed for William Leake, ... 1610.

........Two Sermons ... with a Prayer for the morning therevnto adioyned. And publiſhed by a more perfect Coppie then heere-to-fore. ... Printed by I. R. for William Leake, and are to be ſold at the Grayhound in Paules Churchyard. 1602. [*The Sinners Conuerſion,* and *The Sinners Confeſsion.*]

........[Anr. ed.] ... Printed for William Leake, ... 1605.

........[Anr. ed.] ... Printed for William Leake, ... 1608.

........[Anr. ed.] ... Printed for William Leake, ... 1610.

[Collections of Robert Dexter.]

........Sixe sermons preached ... at Clement Danes Church without Temple barre. And publifhed by a more perfect copie then heretofore. With two prayers of the fame Author hereunto annexed. Printed at London by R. F. for Robert Dexter, ... 1594.

........[Anr. ed.] ... Printed ... by R. F. for Robert Dexter, ... 1594.

........[Anr. ed.] ... Printed by Richard Field for Robert Dexter, ... 1599.

........Ten Sermons ... Printed by Richard Field for Robert Dexter, ... 1596.

........Twelve Sermons ... Printed by Richard Field for Robert Dexter, ... 1598. [6 sermons only.]

Smith, Miles, *Bp.* A learned and godly sermon, preached at Worcefter, at an Afsife: ... At Oxford, Printed by Iofeph Barnes, and are to be fold at Fleet-ftreet at the figne of the Turkes head by Iohn Barnes. 1602.

........Sermons of the right reuerend father in God Miles Smith late Lord Bishop of Glocester. Transcribed out of his originall manuscripts, and now published for the common good. ... Printed by Elizabeth Allde for Robert Allot, ... 1632. [15 sermons, dates not given.]

Smyth, Henry, Certain sermons. Edinburgh. Waldegraue, [1600?] [Not seen.]

Some, Robert. A Godly Sermon preached in Latin at great S. Maries in Cambridge, in Marche 1580. by Robert Some: and tranflated by himfelfe into Engglifh. [sic] ... Imprinted by Henrie Middleton, for George Bifhop. 1580.

Sparke, Thomas. A sermon preached at Cheanies at the buriall of the right honorable the Earle of Bedford, the 14. of September. 1585. ... Imprinted at London. 1585.

........[Anr. ed.] ... Newly perufed and corrected by the Authour. At Oxford, Printed by Iofeph Barnes Printer to the Vniuerfitie. 1594.

........A sermon preached at Whaddon in Buckinghamfhyre the 22. of Nouember 1593. at the buriall of the Right Honorable, Arthur Lorde Grey of Wilton, Knight of the moft Honorable order of the Garter, . . . At Oxford, Printed by Ioseph Barnes Printer to the Vniuerſitie. 1593.

Spenser, John. A learned and gracious sermon at Paules Crosse. G. Purslowe for S. Rande. 1615. [Preached October 10, 1602.] [Not seen.]

Stockwood, John. A sermon Preached at Paules Croſſe on Barthelmew day, being the 24. of Auguſt 1578. Wherin, beſides many other profitable matters meete for all Chriſtians to follow, is at large prooued, that it is the part of all thoſe that are fathers, houſeholders, and Scholemaiſters, to inſtruct all thoſe vnder their gouernmente, in the word and knowledge of the Lorde. . . . Imprinted by Henry Bynneman for George Byſhop. [1578.]

........A very fruiteful Sermon preched at Paules Croſſe the tenth of May laſt, being the first Sunday in Eaſter Terme: in which are conteined very neceſſary and profitable leſſons and inſtructions for this time. . . . Imprinted at London for George Biſhop. 1579. [Printed by Thomas Dawſon.]

........A very fruitfull and neceſſarye Sermon of the moſt lamentable deſtruction of Ieruſalem, and the heauy iudgements of God executed vppon that people for their ſinne and diſſobedience: publiſhed at this time to the wakening and ſtirring vp of all ſuch, as bee lulled aſleepe in the cradle of ſecuritie or careleſneſſe, that they maye at length repente them of their harde hartednes, and contempt of God his word, leaſt they taſte of the like plagues for their rebellion and vnrepentance, not knowing with the wilful inhabitants of Ieruſalem, the daye of their viſitation. . . . Imprinted at London by Thomas Dawſon. 1584.

........A verie godlie and profitable Sermon of the neceſsitie, properties, and office of a good Magiſtrate, and what duety the people dooth owe vnto the ſame: the which may not vnfitlie be tearmed, A preſident for all Incorporations to dyrect them in the Chriſtian choice of a godly Magiſtrate. Printed at London by I. C. for Thomas Butter, . . . 1584.

Tanner, J. A Sermon preached at Paules Croſſe the firſt day of Iune. 1596. . . . Printed by the Widow Orwin for Richard

Ockold, and are to be ſold at the Signe of the Bible in Paules Church-yard. 1596.

Tayler, Frauncis. A Godly, zealous, and learned Sermon, vpon the 18. 19. 20. 21. verſes of the 10. Chap. to the Romaines. Wherein is ſet foorth vnto vs the greate mercy of God in the calling of the Gentiles, and his iuſt iudgemente in the reiecting of the vnbeleeuing Iews, & vs alſo, if we with like obſtinacie contemne his profered mercies. ... Imprinted at London by T. D. for Thomas Woodcocke. 1583.

Temple, Robert. A Sermon teaching diſcretion in matters of religion, and touching certayne abuſes nowe in the Churche: Preached at Paules Croſſe the .21 of Nouember ... Imprinted at London by R. B. for Edward Aggas. 1592.

Thomas, Lewis. Seauen sermons. V. Simms, 1599. [Not seen.]

........[Anr. ed.] Seauen Sermons, or, The Exerciſes of ſeauen Sabbaoths. 1. The Prophet Dauids Arithmetike. 2. Peters Repentance. 3. Chriſts laſt Supper. 4. Chriſt combating with Satan. 5. The Sea-mans Carde. 6. The Sinners Bath. 7. The forming of Eue the firſt woman. Together with a ſhort Treatiſe vpon the Commandements. ... Editio quarta. Printed by Valentine Sims. 1602.

........[Anr. ed.] ... Editio ſeptima. ... Printed by Thomas Purfoot for Valentine Sims. 1610.

Tomkys, John. A sermon preached the 26. day of May. 1584 in S. Maries Church in Shrewesbury; Before the right honorable the Earle of Leiceſter, accompanied with the Earle of Eſſex, the Lorde of the North, diuers Knightes, Gentle-men of worſhypfull callying, the worſhipfull Bayliues, Aldermen and Burgeſſes of the Towne of Salop: ... Now firſt publiſhed by the authour. ... Seen, peruſed, and allowed accordying to her Maiesties Iniunctions. ... Printed by Robert Waldegraue, for William Ponſonby. Anno. 1586.

Topsell, Edward. The reward of religion. Deliuered in ſundrie Lectures vpon the Booke of Ruth, wherein the godly may ſee their daily and outwarde tryals, with the preſence of God to aſsiſt them, and his mercies to recompence them: Verie profitable for this preſent time of dearth, wherein manye are moſt pittifully tormented with want; and alſo worthie to bee confidered in this Golden age of the preaching of the word, when fome vomit vp the loathfomnes therof, and others fall away to damnable fecuritie. ... Seene and allowed. ... Printed by Iohn Windet. 1596. [17 lectures.]

........[Anr. ed.] ... Printed by Iohn Windet. 1597.

[Anr. ed.] ... Printed by Iohn Windet. 1601.

........Times lamentation: or An expofition on the prophrt Ioel, in fundry Sermons or Meditations. ... Printed by Edm. Bollifant, for George Potter. 1599. [42 sermons.]

Trigge, Francis. A godly and fruitfull sermon preached at Grantham. Anno. Dom. 1592. ... Wherein as in a glaffe, every degree may plainely fee their fpots and ftaines: and may bee thereby made in deede beautifull (if they doe not hate to be reformed) againft the appearance of Iefus Chrift. At Oxford. Printed by Ioseph Barnes. 1594.

........[Anr. ed.] ... Oxford, Ioseph Barnes, 1597. [Not seen.]

Turnbull, Richard. [part 1] An exposition vpon the cononicall epistle of Saint Iames: with the tables, Analyfif, and refolution, both of the whole Epiftle, and euery Chapter thereof: with the particular refolution of euery fingular place. Diuided into 28. lectures or sermons: . . . Imprinted at London by Iohn Windet. 1591. [part 2] An exposition vpon the Canonicall Epiftle of Saint Iude: With the Analyfif and refolution, both generall of the whole Epiftle, and particular of euerie Lecture: Diuided into tenne Sermons or Lectures, ... Imprinted by Iohn Windet, 1591. [part 3] An exposition vpon the XV Psalm deuided into foure sermons. Compiled by Richard Turnbull, ... as they were preached at Pauls Croffe, when as at feueral times he was called thereunto. ... Imprinted at London by Iohn Windet. 1591. [42 sermons.]

........[Anr. ed.] [part 1] ... Newly corrected, enlarged, and amended by the authour. Imprinted at London by Iohn Windet. 1592. [part 2] ... and lately reuifed and augmented by the Authour. ... Imprinted by Iohn Windet, 1592. [part 3] ... Now lately perufed, corrected and augmented by the Authour. ... Imprinted at London by Iohn Windet. 1592. [42 sermons.]

......[Anr. ed.] [parts 1 and 2 together] ... Imprinted at London by Iohn Windet, and are to be folde by Richard Bankworth, ... 1606. [38 sermons.]

[part 3] ... [Windet for Bankworth 1606?] [Title-page wanting.] [4 sermons on Psalm 15.]

Tyrell, Anthony. A fruitfull sermon preached in Chrifts-Church the 13. of Iulie. Anno. 1589. By Anthony Tyrell fometime a Seminarie Prieft. But by the great mercie of God made a true profeffor of the Gofpel, and Preacher of his holy word; conteining an admonition vnto vertue, and a dehortation from vice. Taken by Characterye. ... Printed by Iohn Windet, and are to be fold by Abraham Kitfon. [1589.]

Tyrer [or Tryer], Ralph. Five godlie sermons, Preached by R. T. bachiler of diuinitie. 1. The Charge of the Cleargie. 2. The Crowne of Chriftians. 3. The annointment of Chrift, or Chriftian ointment. 4. A feftiuall Sermon vpon the Natiuitie of Chrift. 5. The fruits of hypocrifie. ... Printed by I. H. for Iohn Harifon. 1602.

Udall, John. Amendment of life: three sermons, vpon Actes 2. verses 37. 38. conteining the true effect of the worde of God, in the conuerfion of the godly: and the maner how it changeth their harts, and reformeth their liues, which is the true worke of regeneration. ... Imprinted for Thomas Man, W. B. and N. L. 1584.

........ [Anr. ed.] ... Printed by Robert Walde-graue, for T. Man, and T. Gubbins. Anno. 1588.

........ Certaine sermons, taken out of seuerall places of Scripture. ... Printed by Adam Iflip, for Thomas Man. 1596. [19 sermons.]

........ The combate betwixt Christ and the Deuill. Foure Sermons vpon the temptations of Chrift in the wildernes by Sathan, wherein are to be fene the fubtile fleightes that the tempter vfeth agaynft the children of God, and the meanes that God hath appointed to refifte him, fanctified to our vfe in the example of our Sauiour Iesus Christ. ... Printed by Robert Walde-graue, for Thomas Man, and William Brome. [1588?]

........ [Anr. ed.] ... Thomas Orwin, for Thomas Man, and Thomas Gubbin. 1589.

........ Obedience to the Gofpell. Two sermons, conteining fruteful matter, both of doctrine, and exhortation: very needefull to be knowne, and practifed in thefe our dayes: vpon the words of the holy ghoft, written by the Euangelift S. Luke, chapter 2. verfes 15. 16. 17. 18. 19. 20. conteining the effect of the birth of Christ, (reuealed by the Angell of God) in the fheepeherds, and others that heard of it. Gathered out of the Sermons of Iohn Vdall, ... and publifhed at the requeft of fome of them that heard them preached. ... Imprinted for T. Man, W. B. and N. L. 1584.

........[Anr. ed.] ... Imprinted by Thomas Orwin for T. Man. 1588.

........Peters Fall. Two Sermons vpon the Hiftorie of Peters denying Chrift. Wherin we may fee the caufes of mans falling from God, and the manner how both the wicked thorough incredulitie and of the godly by infirmitie: and alfo the way that God hath fet downe in his word to rife againe. ... Prouerbs. 24. 16. A iuft man falleth feauen times, and rifeth againe, but the wicked fall into mifchiefe. Printed at London by Iohn Windet, and Thomas Iudfon for Nicholas Lyng. Anno. 1584.

........[Anr. ed.] ... Printed for Thomas Man, ... [1590?]

........The true remedie againft Famine and warres. Fiue Sermons vpon the firfte chapter of the prophefie of Ioel, wherein the Councell that the holy Ghoste gaue the Ifraelites to redreffe the famine which they felt, and preuent the warres that were threatened to come vpon them; is applied in particular vnto our prefent time: Preached in the time of the dearth. 1586. ...Printed by Robert Walde-graue, for T. Man, and T. Gubbins. [1588.]

W., A. A Fruitfull and Godly Sermon, preached at Paules crofse before the Honourable audience and affemblie there, this prefent yeare 1592. Vpon the 5. chapter of the prophefie of Zacharie, 1, 2, 3, 4, verfes. By A. W. ... Printed at London by R. B. for Thomas Man, ... [1592.]

Wakeman, Robert. Ionahs sermon, and Ninevehs repentance. A sermon preached at Pauls Croffe Jun. 20. 1602. and now thought fit to be publifhed for our meditations in thefe times. ...The fecond Impreffion. ... Printed at Oxford by Iofeph Barnes, and are to be fold ... by Simeon Waterfon. 1606.

Walsall, John. A Sermon Preached at Pauls Croſſe by Iohn Walſal, ... 5. October. 1578. And publiſhed at the earneſt requeſt of certaine godlie Londoners and others. ... Printed for G. Byſhop. [1578.]

Wentworth, Peter. A sermon faithfullie and trulie publiſhed: According as it was preached at the Courte, at Greenewiche, the Tweſday in Eaſter weeke, before the Right honorable and diligent Auditory. ... Printed by Iohn Windet, for Tho. Gubbin, and Iohn Winnington. 1587.

Westerman, William. Two sermons of assise: The one intituled; A prohibition of Reuenge: The other, A Sword of Maintenance. Preached at two ſeuerall times, before the Right worſhipfull Iudges of Aſſiſe, and Gentlemen aſſembled in Hertford, for the execution of iustice: and now publiſhed. ... Printed by R. B. for Gregory Seaton, ... 1600.

Westfaling, Herbert, *Bp.* A Treatiſe of reformation in religion, diuided into ſeuen Sermons preached in Oxeford, ... Hereunto are added two ſermons touching the ſupper of the Lorde. ... Seene and allowed. Londini impen. Geor. Byſhop. 1582. [Printed by Thomas Dawson.]

Whitaker, William. Cygnea cantio Guilielmi Whitakeri, hoc est, ultima illius concio ad clerum. habita Cantabrigiæ in templo Beatæ Mariæ, paulo ante mortem. Octob. 8. An. Dom. 1595. Cantabrigiæ, ex officina Iohannis Legat. 1599.

White, Peter. A Godlye and fruitefull Sermon againſt Idolatrie: Wherein the foolishe diſtinctions and falſe interpretations of the ſeconde commandement, and other ſcriptures pretended by the Papiſts, are plainly and fully confuted: Preached the .xv. daye of Ianuarie. 1581. In the Parriſhe Church of Eaton Sooken, within the Countie of Bedforde, By P. W. ... Imprinted by Frauncis Coldocke. 1581.

White, Richard. Orationes Duæ. Londini apud Reginaldum Wolfium 1566. [Title-page wanting.]

White, Thomas. A godlie Sermon preached the xxi. day of Iune, 1586. at Penſehurſt in Kent, at the buriall of the late Right honourable Sir Henrie Sidney Knight of the noble order of the Garter, Lord Preſident of Wales, and of her Maieſties

Moſt honourable priuie Councell. ... Printed by Henrie Midleton. M.D.LXXXVI.

........A sermon Preached at Pawles Croſſe on Sunday the ninth of December. 1576. [1577?] by T. W. Imprinted at London by Francis Coldock. 1578.

........A sermõ Preached at Pawles Croſſe on Sunday the thirde of Nouember 1577. in the time of the Plague, by T. W. Imprinted at London by Francis Coldock. 1578.

........A Sermon Preached at Paules Croſſe the 17. of Nouember An. 1589. In ioyfull remembrance and thanksgiuing vnto God, for the peaceable yeres of her Maieſties most gratious Raigne ouer vs, now 32. ... Printed by Robert Robinſon and Thomas Newman. 1589.

Whitgift, John, *Abp.* A godlie Sermon preched before the Queenes Maieſtie at Grenewiche the .26. of March laſt paſt, ... Seene and allowed according to the order appoynted. ... Imprinted at London by Henry Bynneman, for Humphrey Toy. Anno. 1574.

........A Moſt godly and Learned Sermon, Preached at Pauls Croſſe the 17 of Nouember, in the yeare of our Lord. 1583. Maledici Regnum Dei non poſſidebunt. 1. Cor. 6. 10. ... Imprinted at London by Thomas Orwin, for Thomas Chard. 1589.

Wilcox, Thomas. The summe of a sermon, preached at Sowthell the thirtith of March. 1596. By T. W. ... Printed by the Widow Orwin, for Thomas Man. 1597.

Williams, John. De Christi iustitia, et in regno spirituali ecclesiæ pastorum officio. Concio Ad Academicos Oxonienſes. ... Oxoniæ, Ex officina Typographica Ioſephi Barneſii. 1597.

Worship, William. The Christians mourning garment. The third Edition. ... Printed for Thomas Pauier ... 1603.

........[Anr. ed.] ... Printed for Thomas Pauier, ... 1608.

........[Anr. ed.] ... Printed for T. P. 1610.

Yonger, William. A sermon preached at great Yarmouth, Vpon Wedneſday, the 12. of September. 1599. By W. Y. The argument whereof was choſen to miniſter inſtructions vnto the people vpon occaſion of thoſe preſent troubles, which then were feared by the Spaniards. ... Imprinted at London by Simon Stafford, ... 1600.

........[Anr. ed.] ... Imprinted at London by Simon Stafford: and are to be ſold by Thomas Man. 1600. [Not in S. T. Cat.; Bodl. 8vo. D. 53. Th.]

Young, John, *Bp.* A sermon preached before the Queenes Maieſtie, the ſecond of March, An 1575. ... Imprinted at London, by Rycharde Watkins. Cum Priuilegio. [1576?]